EVERYMAN

AND HIS

COMMON STOCKS

EVERYMAN

AND HIS

COMMON STOCKS

A Study of Long Term Investment Policy

By

L<small>AURENCE</small> H. S<small>LOAN</small>

Vice President, Standard Statistics Co., Inc.; Author of
"Security Speculation—The Dazzling Adventure"
and "Corporation Profits "

WHITTLESEY HOUSE

M<small>c</small>GRAW-HILL BOOK COMPANY, INC.

NEW YORK AND LONDON

1931

Published by
WHITTLESEY HOUSE
A Division of the
McGRAW-HILL BOOK COMPANY, INC.

*Printed in the United States of America by
the Maple Press Company, York Pa.*

To

C. A. P.

FRIEND AND PRECEPTOR,
THESE MANY DATA

CONTENTS

I. INTRODUCTION

II. VALUE-MAKING FORCES

III. PRICE-MAKING FORCES

I
INTRODUCTION

1. SURVEY OF THE FIELD

The literature of investment grows apace.

Not so rapidly as the physical volume of investment certificates available to the public, of course, and assuredly not so rapidly as the public's desire to profit by investment knowledge. (The secular trend of the curve of acquisitive desire would appear to have a steeper upward slope than any other which one encounters in the study of economic phenomena; where the trends of population growth and of the volume of physical production are lowly worms, creeping painfully upward at the rate of only a few per cent per year, the pitch of the acquisitive desire trend line may be thought of as a care-free eagle, forever soaring, soaring upward into the illimitable roof of the universe.)

But even so, the help that the printed word has been able to give to those who seek investment knowledge has been very considerable; of especially striking significance have been the contributions of the past few years.

Something over a full decade ago this writer conceived it to be to his purpose to look through, with some care, virtually all of the then available volumes dealing with American investment problems. The most striking facts which emerged from the survey were these:

a. After elimination of the doings of ignorant and illiterate commentators, of those whose work was argumentative in that it sought to persuade one to a special viewpoint, and of those who apparently misstated facts with great deliberateness and drew from these misstatements palpably false conclusions, hardly more than a score of authoritative, trustworthy works on investment matters remained.

b. These dealt for the most part with securities bearing a fixed income. Common stocks were rather generally, although of course not altogether, avoided. The dominating feeling seemed to be that this class of securities constituted a medium not sufficiently respectable to engage (publicly) the attention of reputable economists.

c. Such volumes on investment as were available, say a decade and a quarter ago, were greatly inadequate in their coverage of the field. There were many aspects of the subject, both essential and basic, upon which there were no printed sources of reference whatsoever.

d. This available literature was long on description and short on analysis. General principles were touched upon with a light hand. There were few who had the courage to leave upon the printed page a definite and clear-cut forecast as to future probabilities. Indeed, economic forecast itself was then most frequently referred to as "prophecy," and most economists and statisticians who spoke audibly hastened to disclaim either an effort or the ability to estimate the future.

A relatively brief span of years has wrought great change, not only in the physical volume of books on investment matters, but in the character- istics of the material that has been recently pre- sented for public consumption.

There has developed a much more adequate coverage of the field. Common stocks have received the lion's share of attention. Basic principles have been developed, critically examined, openly and courageously endorsed or damned. Methods of the higher statistics have been freely used as tools in probing for truth. Forecast has been publicly acknowledged as an essential and inescapable part of the problem. The significance of cyclical phe- nomena has been recognized, and their implications frankly dealt with.

But the literature of investment, despite its growth and improvement, retains one outstanding characteristic: disorganization.

This is perhaps inevitable, due to the fact that investment itself is still far from an exact science, and more especially due to the circumstance that those who are continuously attacking the subject in the spirit of true economic research, and who go to the pains to make their findings a part of the written record, roam through a fertile valley as lone wolves, pausing to devour those data which are to their particular taste, to attack those segments of the whole which may be of dominating interest to them, or which it may be to their advantage to attack.

Therein lies no basis for criticism. No one, even should he be an economist general in command of the services of scores and scores of subordinates, could hope to cover thoroughly, or to report publicly upon, the entire problem. It is much too big. The interest of public knowledge would appear to be much better served by intensive attacks and careful reports upon minute sections of the whole, than by general and inconclusive converging movements against a far-flung front.

There is no pontifex to direct, or control, or coordinate the efforts of all those who labor in the search of investment truth; none to say with authority to Research Workers A, B, C, D, X, etc.:

"Thou shalt labor for five years studying the relationship of bond prices and interest rates;

"And thou shalt labor a similar period of time studying the relationship of bond prices and commodity prices;

[6]

"And thou shalt labor with bond prices and the trend of corporation earnings;

"And thou with common stock prices and money rates;

"And thou with price-earnings ratios;

"And thou with cyclical phenomena" . . . etc.

Hence disorganization is inescapable; it doubtless will persist far into the future. Likewise is incompleteness inescapable, although it tends to lessen as the sheer physical volume of the available literature grows.

Now, for purposes of our immediate interest, the point of all the foregoing is simply this:

The literature of investment, despite its increasing adequacy and reliability, is highly specialized and greatly particularized. It tends to concentrate upon a relatively few aspects of the problem, rather than to spread itself evenly over the whole field. Necessarily it tends to report the observations and conclusions of specific individuals, or of specific research groups.

It therefore becomes the very essence of sound policy that, when anyone assumes the responsibility for making a public report on any aspect of the investment problem, he shall take the utmost care to *identify the sector upon which he proposes to operate, and to define clearly the limitations of his work*. Failure to do so is likely not only to confuse the reader, but actually to mislead him.

[7]

Hence the obligation to define and delimit in the present case:

It is the purpose of this book to deal somewhat more with the generalities of common stock investment problems than with the particulars. No one aspect of the situation will be given intensive nor exhaustive attention. Rather, it is the plan to survey the field broadly, and to work toward *general* conclusions which, it is hoped, may prove helpful in the formulation and prosecution of a *general* long term investment program.

A considerable amount of attention will be directed toward underlying *principles*—toward the identification of these principles, toward their statement, and toward the testing of them.

A vigorous effort will be made to differentiate between obviously valid principles on the one hand and seemingly valid ones on the other, and to indicate the points of fallibility even in those premises which appear to be reasonably sound.

The experiences of the long bull market running from the summer of 1921 to the autumn of 1929, and of the subsequent major bear swing in stock prices, will be utilized to the fullest extent that is practical.

Throughout, the viewpoint will be that of the *long term* investor. The "long term," for our present purposes, will be a period of a year or more—

perhaps five years, ten, twenty, a lifetime, several consecutive lifetimes. (This definition will stand only for the time being; it will be amended later to an important degree.) An "investor" will be one who purchases securities of any type with the intention, all other things being equal, of retaining what he has bought for a year or more, *i.e.*, for the long term. In other words, the time limit of the security purchaser's intent defines his status as between a speculator and an investor.

Obviously, these definitions are rigidly arbitrary. It would be difficult to defend them under certain circumstances. But recall that they are definitions "for our present purposes." Other analysts may have other purposes, and therewith other definitions. Probably no terms in the English language are used more loosely or with greater flexibility than the two (long term and investor) which we have here sought to define. The main advantage of an attempt at definition, therefore, is that it should at least avoid confusion and uncertainty. That, when one is dealing with terms which are habitually uncertain in their implications, should constitute at least a step toward clarity.

Thus having taken the first fatal step in the quicksand of lexicography, it will be just as well to take another without pause.

More in the interest of economizing words and explanatory phrases, securities and insecurities

[9]

alike will be referred to as "securities." Common stocks, preferred stocks and bonds will all be tossed into the same hopper for the purpose of identifying a broad class of financial instruments. Thus the term security as here used does not describe but merely identifies. Expressed another way, a security, for our present purpose, will be assumed to be any certificate of ownership in an incorporated business enterprise, or any marketable certificate of creditorship to such an incorporated business enterprise, or to the equivalent of a federal, state, or municipal government.

Our concern here, however, will be almost altogether—say 99 per cent—with the common stock section of the investment portfolio. The senior security sections of the portfolio will be considered in a later study.

It will further be assumed that the long term security owner with whom we will be discussing pertinent matters is, in virtually all cases, both an absentee and minority partner. It is very important that this assumption be emphatically stated, because it implies that our investor has available only the usual published sources of information.

It will *not* be assumed that our investor knows as little about securities and their markets as the average bond salesman, or as the average elevator operator or truck driver, or as a person who consistently breaks 80 on 18 holes of golf. Nor will it, on the other hand, be assumed that his knowledge of security market matters is equivalent to that of the so-called professional, who, over a period of years, has been able to give his entire attention (or at least the major portion of it) to the intensive study and analysis of security market phenomena.

In the absence of these two assumptions it would in the first place be insulting to our hypothetical reader's intelligence were what follows to take the form of a primer or even an elementary essay on investment practice, while similarly it would be needlessly imposing upon his energy and his time to offer him for consumption a highly complex and strictly technical treatise. Hence we shall be more anxious to avoid involved and unclear statements of facts than to side-step difficult conceptions and ideas.

Stated in another way, the investor for whose consideration we here propose to present certain facts, deductions, and opinions is the average business-man investor: one who is safely over the earlier and preparatory stages of the problem, but whose time has been so fully engaged in other matters that he has not had the opportunity to give his investment program all of the study which its importance deserves—who still, perchance, has something more to learn about investment phenomena, and who is in a mood to be told that, no matter how diligently he strives, there will be something else, and something else, and yet something else, still to be learned.

And, as previously intimated, the objective of all this ado will be to emerge, *enfin*, with a body of definite conclusions which it is hoped may be of aid to those who are seeking to formulate and carry out a conservative long term common stock investment program.

2. A WORKMAN AND HIS TOOLS

A carpenter does not set out to build a house with his bare hands alone, nor a dentist to fill a tooth, nor a chemist to work through an experiment, nor an engineer to map out a railroad line.

Each must have his tools, and, if these are to prove effective, the workman must possess both a certain amount of experience in their use, and a certain knowledge of their functions and distinguishing characteristics.

Weird and heretical as the idea may seem to many persons, intelligent long term investment (and even intelligent speculation, with which we are not here concerned) implies precisely the same things: tools with which to work; a knowledge of their use and capabilities. Much more often than not it will be found that the most serious tragedies in the investment markets befall those who enter upon their task the least well equipped for it.

Unhappily, even the informed investors are almost certain to meet many grievous disappointments over a period of time. That is an element which is inherent in the security markets themselves, continuously and inevitably. *But we take the position, without any essential reservation, that both the frequency and the violence of the normal security market hazard tend to increase or decrease in direct ratio with the number of the investor's tools, and his competency to use them.*

The five most essential tools which the investor will find it to his purpose to understand and utilize are:

Accounting.
Statistics.
Economic analysis.
Forecast.
Recurring sources of factual information, and especially of interim information.

There is intended no intimation here that a high degree of expertness is absolutely necessary in the use of these tools by the average investor. A working knowledge of them will ordinarily suffice. Yet it cannot be forgotten that it is the best technician who builds the most successfully, the most enduringly. Increasing knowledge of the tools of security market analysis over a period of time can assuredly do no harm; this writer holds that it can do nothing in the world but enhance the probability of attaining more satisfactory results.

In the paragraphs immediately following, the tools of security analysis which have been named will be discussed quite briefly—so briefly that their significance will be no more than suggested. Their applicability to investment facts will be dealt with more in detail as the argument progresses.

ACCOUNTING

Accounting is a medium by which business concerns control and compute the results of their operations. The record of these results is made public in the form of income accounts and balance sheets, which, taken singly or together, are commonly called "financial statements."

A financial statement is strictly an accounting document. It is prepared by an accountant; it is computed and drawn up according to the rules, practices, and technique generally recognized as valid by the accounting profession—such as they are.

At the same time, the financial statement (annual, semi-annual, quarterly, or monthly) is in most cases the only *official* evidence that comes into the security owner's possession to tell him of the results that have been achieved by the concern in which he has a financial interest. True, unofficial statements, which might be called editorial statements rather than financial ones, are from time to time allowed to become public by the executives of incorporated business concerns, and often such statements are of great help.

[15]

But these extraneous statements cannot be relied upon to appear with any degree of regularity. There is no obligation upon the corporate management to issue them. The financial statement *can* be relied upon to appear at stated periods, and indeed must be issued to security owners if a given concern's securities are listed upon any of the larger exchanges.

The intelligent and careful security owner will check through the financial statement as soon as it becomes available to him, in an effort to help himself decide the eternal question as to whether his holdings of a particular issue should be retained, increased, or disposed of. The intelligent and careful purchaser who is contemplating a new commitment will consult the latest official financial statements available before he makes his choice.

Both current and prospective purchasers will consult and analyze.

They cannot even consult intelligently unless they understand the rudiments of accounting practice. Assuredly they can get nowhere whatsoever with analysis if they lack such knowledge.

Expressed in another way, a security owner must be able to "read" a financial statement if he hopes to make wise decisions. He must be able to follow it through, step by step, reading between the lines and forming his own independent conclusions as he goes along. He should be able to detect understatement of probable fact on the one hand (concealment of current or prospective value) and overstatement or chicanery on the other hand.

He can do none of these things if he knows not what accountancy is all about, if he is untutored in its way and practices. He need not be an expert accountant himself. What he needs, indeed what he must have, is the mental equipment and the background to understand the published results of the accountant's work. Without this equipment he is a simple child, wandering aimlessly and hopelessly in the dark. Only luck—really a rare thing in a practical, workaday world inhabited by so many who possess expert knowledge—can save him from ultimate disaster.

We assume it is needless to point out here that a working knowledge of the practices of accountancy, and a willingness to check recurrently the published results of accountancy, constitute only one of the tools of security analysis. The work of the accountant, as it is revealed to the financial-minded public at large, is after the fact. Too often it is the barn door that is locked after the horse has been let out. Many, many times the things that the security owner needed to know to protect his position have occurred, and have been discounted market-wise, long before the official financial statement becomes a matter of public record.

[17]

But that does not for an instant relieve the investor from the necessity for utilizing the official financial statement to the full extent of its possibility. Always and under every circumstance this statement must be the starting point in the analysis. Other tools are brought into play as the analysis progresses.

STATISTICS

Chemistry is one of the chief sciences employed by industry to change the form and character of things; to transform raw materials into useful consumers' goods.

Cattle hides, for example, subjected to certain chemical processes, become leather. Iron becomes steel. Other ores are dissolved into their constituent and basic parts. Crude oil becomes gasoline, kerosene, lubricants, etc. A series of exposures upon a spool of film becomes a reel of motion pictures.

Statistics are the chemistry of arithmetic. By the use of statistics, one treats raw arithmetic data, and often changes them into more useful forms.

A formidable term, statistics! One implying a difficult and highly technical extension of mathematics into realms of calculations so complex and involved as to be well-nigh unintelligible to the layman. But that is not the sense in which the word is used here. In referring to statistics as an essential tool in security analysis, it is our thought merely to suggest that something more than bare mathematical facts, as they are set forth in official financial statements, is desirable.

A few paragraphs earlier, reference was made to the necessity of reading between the lines of the average financial statement. One might have said "dig" between the lines. Statistics provide the tool with which one digs . . . with which one discovers relationships . . . gives mathematical values to these relationships . . . computes and detects the true significance of mathematical facts . . . reveals comparisons and contrasts . . . produces derived data that are highly helpful.

Statistics function as a searchlight. By their use one reveals and illuminates.

Statistical practice is applicable to business facts equally with security market facts. The same instrumentality is used to bring the two sets of data into focus, so that they may be viewed side by side, compared and contrasted.

And in the popular sense of the term, statistics signify, in addition to the treatment of data, the recording and preservation of data over a period of time. Utilized in this fashion, statistics function as the historian of security market and business mathematics. It is from historical data (the more complete and comprehensive the better!) that one sets forth toward a calculation of future possibilities.

Graphic statistics are especially helpful in the visualization of mathematical facts. In Wall Street the student who persistently translates his statistics into graphic form, and who bases his decisions as to future action wholly or largely upon the historic behavior of his curves, is called a "chart reader." His charts tell him what to do. His methods are empirical. He is commonly looked upon as a quack; perhaps rightly so, more often than not.

We are not here concerned with the statistical efforts of the chart reader, but rather with those of the "chart looker"—the investor who uses charts to visualize various sets of data that he wishes to study, and who considers statistical data portrayed in this form merely as a convenience in working out a conception. The chart looking habit, once formed, makes not only for promptness in arriving at results, but often for accuracy and for an enlarged viewpoint.

The investor who is bored by statistics (graphic or tabular), who has neither the ability to utilize the simpler statistical processes himself nor to understand the statistical work of others, marches partially blindfolded to his appointed station among the security market derelicts.

The intelligent and careful investor will take every reasonable step to acquaint himself with the kit of statistical tools which are most frequently employed by advanced students of security market data; to understand the methods of their employment and the significance of their revelations.

In other words, the investor who is bored by statistics, or who has not the mental capacity for mastering the elementary statistical processes most frequently utilized in treating security market data, has no business being an investor at all. He should be sheerly a saver, and let others do his thinking for him.

ECONOMIC ANALYSIS

We must define our terms as we go along and often even take great liberties with what was once their orthodox standing.

"Economic analysis," as it is here conceived, is that process of reasoning which works from broad, general business facts to specific security market situations.

Say that commodity prices on the average have been declining for six months past. What is the likely effect of this movement upon the types of securities which A owns?

The aggregate volume of production in the United States increases, over a period of time, from index 110 to index 125. How is this phenomenon to be translated into terms of security market behavior in the aggregate, and specifically into terms of *A's* particular portfolio?

The rediscount rate at the Federal Reserve Bank of New York is raised to 5½ per cent; then to 6 per cent; then to 6½ per cent. What does this portend?

Bank loans steadily increase over a period of time. The rate on call loans rises correspondingly. The volume of new construction shrinks. Copper prices fall. A new and more prolific process for recovering gasoline from crude oil is discovered and widely adopted.

The Canadian wheat crop fails. The Mediterranean fly multiplies in Florida as the boll weevil dies in Texas. Scrap steel at Chicago is in oversupply.

The Administration at Washington issues a statement, assuring us that everything is all O.K. New model Fords roll off the assembly line at Dearborn at the rate of ten thousand units a day. Women confess the error of the ways of the short skirt, and return to the long one. It becomes impossible to let first class apartments in large cities unless their kitchens are equipped with mechanical refrigeration. Al Jolson is a flop in *Mamma's Boy*, upon which the producer's have spent half a million (they assert). A certain Mr.

Hatry in London cuts capers and fails for five million pounds sterling. One of the largest silk reelers in Japan is unable to meet its obligations, and the Tokio stock exchange shuts up shop.

What do all of these events, as they develop and are reported in the public press, mean to the security markets in the large and to the particular securities which *A* chances to be holding? And what should *A* do about it?

Economic analysis is the interpretation of general business facts, with a reasonable degree of accuracy, and the application of this interpretation to the more microscopic individualities.

Economic analysis is continuous. It is carried on while one is waiting for the exact (so to speak) information that will ultimately be contained in the official corporation financial statement. Correctly reasoned through, it often means the difference between devastating loss or handsome gains on the one hand, and moderate ones on the other.

It is an indispensable tool of security analysis.

FORECAST

Prophecy has always been a rather disreputable sort of business. Not unaccountably, the opprobrium associated with the practice of prophecy attaches also to business forecast.

[23]

Thus many of our business leaders, when they are called upon by the financial editors at the beginning of each year to look into the future and give the populace the benefit of their opinions, are in most cases careful to preface their statements with the declaration that they do not pose as prophets.

Numerous financial periodicals, as well as the financial sections of practically all the daily newspapers, studiously avoid any reference to future probabilities, unless, as the slang phrase has it, they "can pin it on someone"; that is, quote someone, so it will be the other fellow rather than the periodical itself that is wrong if things do not turn out as expected.

Publicly at least, one encounters on every hand a shyness about outright forecasting that in many cases amounts to nothing less than downright nonsense.

The truth of the matter is that no business concern can be intelligently conducted unless its policies are directly and firmly geared to the management's business forecasts. And it is equally true that the effectiveness of any business enterprise is in direct ratio to the forecasting ability of that enterprise's management.

The majority of important business decisions, in other words, are made with an eye on tomorrow's probabilities. The correctness with which tomorrow's probabilities are calculated give validation to today's decisions.

Credit which is extended by the commercial banker today is not paid back today or yesterday. Obviously it cannot be; the borrower pays tomorrow. The banker forecasts that he will be able to pay; that his individual earnings or his concern's profits during the future will enable him to pay.

The manufacturer or merchandiser purchases supplies today to be sold tomorrow. He forecasts the volume that he can sell, and the price at which he can sell. If he did not do so, he would have no way of determining the volume he would buy, or the price he would pay today.

The manufacturer enlarges his facilities—adds floor space and new equipment to his plant. He does so because he has calculated that he can sell a greater volume of goods tomorrow than he is selling today.

A railroad runs a line into a sparsely settled territory, knowing that the capital expense involved cannot be justified today, but assuming that it can be justified tomorrow as population increases.

The telephone company, the gas company, and the electric light company extend their facilities to the new suburban development—not after that development has reached its maximum of growth, but while it is still an infant. Capacity of the phone cables, and the gas mains and the electric lines are excessive at the beginning. But such capacity as is provided is based upon a forecast of future growth. If this forecast is over-optimistic, substantial losses are ultimately incurred; similarly if it is over-conservative, because in that event the job is to be done all over again.

No branch of American business, incidentally, gives more attention to business forecast than the utilities.

The American Telephone and Telegraph Company, for example, spends each year millions and millions of dollars on the long term forecasts developed by its economic research departments. The probable growth of every important territory is calculated with mathematical precision. Not only are cables laid on the basis of these forecasts, but manufacturing facilities are provided to produce the equipment that will be needed in the future. And that is the reason—and the sole reason— why, in normal times, you can get a telephone installed in your home within a few days after you have applied for service.

The telephone company has looked ahead. It has not prophesied. It has applied the sciences of statistics and economic analysis to obvious business facts, and has projected reasonable future prob-

[26]

abilities on the basis of these facts. A series of important blunders in forecast would have two immediate results: service would be curtailed, and it would cost the user more money.

If careful forecast is necessary in every line of business, it is equally necessary—perhaps even more so if that were possible—in every security-market program.

The security purchaser cannot escape the obligation to forecast two important elements: the future value of the issue that he holds, and its future price. This is true for the very simple reasons that (*a*) his income from the security that he owns is not received today, but will be received over a series of tomorrows; (*b*) he will not be selling that security today, but tomorrow.

The security purchaser who buys without forecasting is a stupid purchaser. Lacking the forecast, there can be no possible purpose in buying.

Business forecast is not prophecy. It is not guess. It is not "playing a hunch." It is the calculation of reasonable future probabilities, on the basis of all the factual information that can be assembled, and by employing the methods which careful workers in business and security market data have been developing over a period of many years.

At the risk of tedium, we assert once more that intelligent forecast is the very essence of effectiveness in security market operation. We lay it down as a principle from which there is no escape that no security purchase should be carried out in the absence of a careful value and price forecast, and that no forecast should be attempted until there has been assembled a volume of data sufficient to lift that forecast far, far above the level of prophecy or guess.

RECURRING SOURCES OF FACTUAL INFORMATION

Sweet would be the lot of the capitalists in an acquisitive society which had developed its forecasting methods to the point of infallibility. In this circumstance, one could make one's forecast, be sure it was right, and permanently close up shop . . . to spend the rest of one's life leisurely casting for speckled trout, or sunning one's self on the Riviera.

Unhappily, it does not work out this way. Between every individual and his tomorrow a veil is drawn. There are ways by which this veil can be penetrated to some extent. (If it is to one's purpose to penetrate, then to penetrate to some extent is better than not to penetrate at all.)

But after all, tomorrow is the great unknown. The day after tomorrow is an even greater unknown. A year from tomorrow, five years, ten, twenty, become the maximum unknown.

That is to say, the farther ahead one is obliged to project one's business or security market forecast, the more insecure, the more tentative, that forecast becomes.

Thus there devolves the necessity for *reforecast.* The existing forecast (the latest one) must be continuously re-examined and rechecked. It must be reviewed in the light of progressive developments. Often it must be modified. Not infrequently it must be reversed.

A forecast is G.T.C. In security market operations, it is the essence of the program's effectiveness to cancel the forecast at the right time rather than at the wrong time.

It may be said here, as it will be said several times later and at much greater length, that conservative long term investment and reforecast are not incongruous, but directly compatible.

There is a vast gulf between stubbornness and wisdom. A security purchaser does not make himself conservative merely by buying with the intention of "holding for twenty years if necessary," or merely by buying a security that he is willing "to put away in his strong box and forget." If he is wise he maintains his position only so long as he continues reasonably certain that his long term forecast remains valid. But he will not hesitate to change his position as he revises his opinions and calculations. It is the long term nature of an economic forecast which gives validity to a long term investment program, and only that. When and if the forecast is revised, certain portions of the investment program itself automatically come up for revision.

Reforecast is based upon the accrual of knowledge. A, B, C and D are facts today; therefore, over a given future period, X is a probable fact. But tomorrow there appears Fact E, previously unknown and unallowed for; the day after tomorrow there appears Fact F, also unallowed for. E and F become modifiers. Z then becomes a more probable future fact than X.

The investor must place himself in a position to learn of Facts E, F, etc., as promptly as they develop, so that he can fit them into the structure of his forecast and make due allowances in his calculations for their effects.

He must, in other words, expose himself to a continuous stream of new information.

The corporations in which he is a partner or to which he is a lender neither assume nor accept the obligation to provide him with this continuous information. Nor should they, as a matter of fact. Many corporations which regularly issue quarterly statements of earnings send only the annual income account to their security holders. The interim reports attain general circulation only through the medium of the newspapers or financial periodicals.

[30]

And even between these interim reports there is a considerable amount of information relative to specific corporations which the prudent security owner will want to have, and which is normally available through outside sources that are generally conceded to be reliable.

Going a step farther, there are constant developments in specific industries which affect, in some degree and either favorably or unfavorably, all of the concerns operating in those lines of business.

And going a step still farther, there is the constantly shifting panorama of general business activity, the tide of intensity rising or falling, the effects in varying degree reflecting themselves promptly in the affairs of individual corporations— expansion and contraction in the aggregate volume of industrial production; changes in the level of commodity prices; essential shifts in the banking structure, etc.

To interpret correctly these countless extraneous events, and to base thereupon an intelligent course of definitive action is, as we have previously pointed out, the function of what we here call economic analysis.

To expose one's self to knowledge of these events as they develop, is to provide the basis for reforecast.

To reforecast is to bulwark a previous forecast.

To act upon a carefully calculated forecast is to act intelligently rather than blindly.

[31]

3. THE AGENDUM OF THE LONG TERM INVESTMENT PROGRAM

Throughout this section and those that follow the viewpoint will be focused almost entirely upon those economic processes known as the accumulation, acquisition, or preservation, of capital.

No apologies for the theme will be made. In any profits economy—and the American economy is strictly a profits one—acquisition becomes an inescapable economic necessity. If we ourselves do not strive for its accomplishment, no one else will do so for us. Regardless of the personal sacrifices involved, a certain amount of progress with the program is obligatory during the season in which the labor of our hands and minds is capable of producing the greatest volume of goods and services; if not, we leave an unwelcome and equally unjust legacy to others—most often, to others less competent to assume it.

Thus, in a profits economy, the storing-up process becomes merely an economic fact in the same sense that the law of supply and demand, the production of goods, prices, interest rates, land values, etc., are economic facts. Those who prattle so insistently about the evils of the material aspects of life simply do not understand the structural economic organization of the society in which they live.

Now, the frame of mind in which a given individual pursues the process of accumulation, and the rules of the game which he lays down and follows, if any, constitute something entirely different from this economic fact in itself.

Happily for the peace of the world and for the material comfort of its average inhabitant, there are those whose acquisitive demands are moderate; who whittle away at their programs in a fashion that takes nothing unjustly from anyone else; who would not for a moment countenance or follow any course of action that meant attainment for self to the detriment of public welfare; who accumulate, in a word, like civilized human beings.

And on the other hand, there are those who accumulate like swine, cutthroats, or burglars.

Between the two extremes there are as many gradations and standards of performance as there are shades of light and darkness between high noon and midnight.

With social problems—motives, personal conduct and standards, the vagaries of human nature —we are not in the slightest here concerned. These matters fall entirely outside the field of economics.

Reference is made to them in passing merely to leave the thought that the necessary act of acquisition is one thing, and the personal or social characteristics of the millions of persons who are obliged to engage in it are quite something else. The two ideas should not be confused.

Only in one essential respect does the social aspect of the problem attach itself to the data with which we are dealing. *The waste of capital is an abhorrent thing.* And we are not thinking of waste in the sense of destruction, but rather in the sense of dissipation.

We consider capital to have been dissipated, or wasted, when it is needlessly lost. It is needlessly lost, in most cases, through ignorance or carelessness. Society gains nothing by such a dissipation, or redistribution. Indeed, under such circumstances it is true more often than not that the one who loses cannot afford to do so; if there is an offsetting gain, it is usually conferred upon one who does not need it, or who has rendered no useful service that entitles him to it.

The waste of accumulated capital resources will be a matter of primary concern to us. It supplies the chief *raison d'être* for this essay. It may as well be frankly confessed at the outset that our interest in helping rich men get richer is very lukewarm, to say the least. The interest in seeing poor and moderate-circumstanced men and their non-producing dependents get less poor is one of considerably more active concern.

For convenience we may think of capital as accruing, for the most part, from two main sources. We shall designate them as:

a. Simple saving.

b. Enterprise.

Simple saving is the process of denying oneself the utilization of a portion of one's income or assets, and of employing the sums so derived with the minimum of risk.

Naturally, in a civilized and economically far-advanced society such as the United States, one does not often find conservatism in simple saving carried so far as the hoarding of currency, as in, say, France or India. The surplus from which the saver abstains is employed so that it yields a certain return, but, as previously stated and to fall within the limits of our definition, with the minimum of risk, although of course there must always be some risk.

Examples:

Life insurance.

Annuities.

Savings bank accounts.

Adequately secured first mortgages on productive real estate.

High grade bonds.

Highest grade preferred stocks.

Simple saving is a slow method of accumulation, but those who are able to pursue it consistently over a period of time seldom see the almshouse, except as they drive past it in their automobiles.

Over a number of years, the average rate of return on high grade bonds runs around 4½ per cent. A sum of money employed to give this return, with interest credited quarterly and thereafter compounded, doubles in about 15½ years.

At 5 per cent, credited quarterly and compounded, money doubles in about 14 years.

At 6 per cent it doubles in 11⅔ years.

And at 7 per cent (which is higher than can be expected with the minimum degree of risk except under the most extraordinary circumstances) money doubles in fractionally less than 10 years.

To most active business men, possessed of all their faculties, in good health, and conscious of the workings of the economic mechanism about them, and especially to those who conceive themselves as being in a position to accept something greater than the minimum of risk, these rates of accrual are judged to be unacceptably slow.

They seek to employ their funds in such a fashion that, in addition to the normal income return that accrues, *there will be the possibility of enhancement of the principal amount.*

To a certain extent, enhancement of principal is possible collateral to a program of simple saving.

Life insurance, for example, pays a handsome return on the insured's investment, to his heirs, if he dies young—an expedient which even the most conservative simple savers are seldom willing to embrace. But of course life insurance does not pay a handsome return to the average insured, because if it did the philanthropy of the insurance companies would soon pave their roadway to the bankruptcy courts. Life insurance on the average is simple saving in one of its most conservative forms; the enhancement in principal which occurs is, on the average, necessarily at a rate somewhat less than the average cumulative return on the best bonds over a period of time.

The value of money itself, that is to say, the purchasing power of money, changes materially over a period of time, as the amount of credit outstanding in the country ebbs and flows, as commodity prices on the average rise and fall.

Assume that $100, the use of which a simple saver denied himself in mid-1920 and deposited in the savings bank, would have purchased, at the then prevailing level of average commodity prices, 60 units of goods. General prices have fallen to

[37]

such an extent since the middle of 1920 that the same sum, withdrawn from the savings bank in mid-1930 and spent, would have purchased around 110 units of goods.

Here is a clear gain in the value of saved money—technically, a capital gain from the saver's standpoint. But the program is not a practical one in any systematic program of saving. The long term results cannot be relied upon with any degree of certainty. And, more important still, few savers can set aside, in periods of excessively high commodity prices, any appreciable surplus. The high prices themselves take care of that.

Capital appreciation in high grade bonds and preferred stocks, in certain periods and under certain circumstances, is much more real in effect, and much more easy to cash in upon.

The two widest upward moves which have occurred in these classes of securities since the beginning of the present century began in the bond market in 1920 and in the preferred stock market a year later. Both major swings terminated early in 1928.

One hundred thousand dollars' worth of high grade bonds purchased at the extreme 1920 low (July) could have sold at the 1928 peak (March) for $128,000.

Similarly, $100,000's worth of high grade preferred stocks purchased at the extreme low in 1921

(August) could have been sold at the 1928 peak (April) for almost $135,000.

Movements of such wide proportions in these two markets do not come as often as once in a decade. They come about once in a generation.

The annual average gain in bond prices, during the abnormal period referred to above, amounted to 3.6 per cent; that for preferred stocks amounted to about 5.2. And remember, of course, that there are downward as well as upward movements in the prices of senior securities from time to time.

During the 6-year–8-month period in which high-grade preferred stocks were registering a maximum gain amounting to 5.2 per cent per annum, the 404 leading *common* stocks used in the Standard Statistics Company's index were registering a price gain *five times as rapid*.

The simple comparison is a story in itself. It tells, more briefly than any number of words could possibly tell, why so many persons feel obligated to try their hands at enterprise in preference to the slower, and safer, simple saving.

Moreover, successful enterprise breeds its own capital as it progresses and it further makes possible employment of borrowed capital. The statistics of the Department of Internal Revenue conclusively demonstrate that the incomes of the great majority of American citizens are so low, year in and year out, that even the maximum of possible abstinence during their productive years yields a sum which, more often than not, is insufficient for the purposes for which it was intended. Here we have a motive for enterprise even more basic that the mere acquisitive habit.

Now, it must be borne in mind that the purchase of common stocks is only one aspect—and perhaps a relatively small one—of that general type of economic activity which we have designated as enterprise. The purchase of a common stock is only the purchase of a fractional partnership in an incorporated business concern—usually by an absentee owner.

A is equally enterprising when he sets himself up—often with the help of his bank or of some kindly disposed friend—as the sole proprietor of a corner grocery store; *B* equally enterprising when he opens a garage; *C* when he purchases and operates his own taxi; Doctor *D* when he buys a block of lots in the new real estate development; Lawyer *E* when he chips in with one of his clients to help finance a new surety bonding agency; Farmer *F* when he buys (so to speak) his neighbor's 160 acres.

In every case, the objective is a corresponding one: the hope of enhancing a capital sum at a rate more rapid than that returned by simple saving.

In a profits economy, little is given away; as the idiom has it, "it's hard to get something for nothing."

Therefore, the larger gains come at a price. They come at the price of an increased risk. It would be preposterous to assume that returns of 8, 10, 15, 20 per cent on a given capital sum could be won by carrying a risk no greater than is carried by the simple saver who is forced to accept 4½ to 6 per cent. If this were true, no one would be stupid enough to accept the lower bracket returns.

The agendum of the long term investor's program, then, sums up briefly as follows:

It should provide for a certain amount of simple saving—varying, say, from 10 per cent up to 99 per cent. This is a strange and unfamiliar doctrine in such days as these; it was even more extraordinary in the mad stock market whirl of 1928–1929. But it is not a revolutionary doctrine.

At the same time, it is assumed that the investment program of those who will be at all interested in the material to be presented later in this book provides for the acceptance, to a considerable degree, of those business risks which hold the *possibility* of returning gains greater than are yielded by simple saving.

This means engaging in business enterprise. For our present purposes (since this study deals only with securities) it means commitment of a portion of surplus funds in common stocks.

The agendum of our hypothetical investor's program, in other words, provides for a combination of simple saving and enterprise, on the assumption that the one must be the complement of the other to make the program complete and effective. But as the perplexities of enterprise are infinitely greater and more complex than those of simple saving, so, correspondingly, will they here receive the major portion of our consideration.

II
VALUE-MAKING FORCES

1. THE BASIS OF VALUE

One of the difficult aspects of a study such as this lies in the utter impossibility of saying all that is to be said—and at the same time making all the necessary qualifications—in a single breath. The physical necessity for proceeding step by step with the exposition, or, in other words, the futility of trying to take the whole subject matter at one bite, often results both in temporary inaccuracies and in confusion as to the concepts that are being dealt with.

This becomes particularly true when we turn attention to the differentiation as between value and price. To draw this distinction in precise terms, and to qualify properly each basic statement as the argument proceeded, would involve a well-nigh interminable discussion in theoretical economics, and one which would here be entirely out of place.

So we must cut the corners short, ignoring many important qualifications, even though this quicker and easier route involves sacrifice of accuracy, at least for the time being.

The important thing to understand is that, in the particular study here under review, *value and price are regarded as two separate things.*

It is of course impossible to separate them entirely, even in one's mind, because price is the only medium in which value, in the economic sense, can be reported. But even so, an effort at differentiation will be worth while, and is especially pertinent in security market analysis.

If systems of assaying values were uniform, and more especially if systems of pricing values were uniform, our perplexities would be considerably alleviated; there would be scant need for nice distinctions. Indeed, it is the lack of uniformity in systems of assaying and pricing—more outstandingly irregular in the security markets than in any other section of the economic structure, perhaps—which produces the necessity for differentiation.

In so far as possible, therefore, let us erase the thought of price from our minds for the time being, and focus attention only upon that underlying element which price seeks to express in financial terms.

We do not get far with our explanation if we start with the statement that by value we mean intrinsic worth, although that is precisely what we do mean, and it is realized full well that every reputable theoretical economist has devoted several pages in his textbook to explaining why this cannot be a sound conception. Perhaps we should

[46]

come a bit nearer an acceptable definition if we conceived value as the worth of a thing under an ideal pricing system—a pricing system which was always correct, which priced our goods at precisely the proper level, no higher and no lower, and which automatically adjusted itself in exactly the right degree as real value changed.

In any event, what we are anxious to do at this time is to get away from that artificial element which is always present in price, and which is especially and violently present in security prices; instead, to focus attention upon the underlying values which security prices seek to express: correctly sometimes, erroneously sometimes.

Looked at through the eyes of the owners, the value of a business enterprise arises from its ability to generate earning power—or profits, in other words, and disbursable profits at that. This becomes particularly the viewpoint of the small fraction, or absentee owner, who quite naturally takes scant satisfaction in the mere technical excellence of the new plant, the superiority of the product, the humane treatment of old employees, the establishment's institutional reputation, etc. These are matters that are, sometimes, very dear to the hearts of the chief owners, or the managing owners. But obviously such things can be of only passing concern to the investor who has never seen the plant or its employees or its products, and whose sole interest arises from the fact that he has commissioned his banker or his broker in Wall Street to buy a hundred shares of the company's stock for his investment portfolio.

Such an investor is thinking—or should be thinking—of the value of the property as an income producing proposition.

From the security market standpoint, value is not a static, but a progressive thing.

Theoretically, then, the most valuable security in the world would be the one which:

a. Produced the largest income in a given year;

b. Increased this income the most rapidly over a period of years; and

c. Sustained this maximum rate of increase for the longest period of time.

This indeed would be the world's premier security, the investor's ideal of the ultimate: the security which represented the greatest intrinsic value when it was purchased, which increased that value more rapidly than any other security, and which kept up the constantly quickening pace, year after year, year after year, *ad infinitum.*

Could any proposition be simpler than this one, or any economic premise be expressed more definitely?

If an enterprise security* be regarded as an income producing instrument (producing income both in the form of dividends and capital appreciation) what characteristic could be more desirable than that the intrinsic value of this security should increase with the utmost rapidity, and should increase eternally? This is the maximum of value.

The fact itself we shall take to be beyond dispute. Bear in mind that we are not talking of simple saving in any of its forms; we are talking of enterprise; of the acceptance of some degree of economic risk in the hope of securing a return more ample than that yielded by simple saving. Investment being one of the principal types of enterprise, investment science therefore becomes the organization of analytical, statistical, and forecast technique in such a fashion that one may pick the so-called "ideal" enterprise securities.

That is, investment science would aim at such an objective if it were a pure science. But of course it is not. It is one of the very practical sciences, indeed bearing the name science only by good-humored sufferance. Let us here accord it this invidious distinction for convenience if for no

* Often called an equity security in the era of equity madness which ended in the autumn of 1929. Prior to that, merely a common stock. Referred to here and occasionally hereinafter as an enterprise security because the term seems adapted to both the trend and the spirit of the argument.

[49]

other good reason. We may then redefine this term more accurately:

As a practical, workaday science, careful investment becomes the development and application of principles which will enable one to choose securities which in certain major characteristics *resemble or approach* the ideal investment, and which at the same time possess some characteristics that in part at least compensate for their obvious deficiencies as contrasted with the ideal.

Stated another way, the ideal enterprise investment (the one possessing the maximum of intrinsic value today, and promising to increase that value with the maximum rapidity *ad infinitum*) does not exist. If it did exist, investment science, with all its courageous efforts to throw off the heavy shackles of today and soar lightly and safely into tomorrow, is not sufficiently developed to enable one to select the ideal investment on any factual basis whatsoever.

Practically, then, the science of investment becomes a study of compromises. We hold the ideal in our minds, even though we know it to be unobtainable; out task is to find the things which resemble the ideal as nearly as possible and which possess some compensating features for what they lack.

And to make the story complete, thus early in the study, it should be added that security selection, important as it is, constitutes only a portion of the task. Unhappily—unhappily because it greatly complicates and enhances the difficulty of the problem—studies in selection must be supplemented by studies in price. The price phase of the problem, however, will receive but scant attention in the immediately following section dealing with value. Our preliminary attention is to be focused upon some of the basic economic factors from which arise those value-making forces that give certain actual securities *some* characteristics in common with those of the ideal.

2. GROSS INCOME

What has been said in the preceding section justifies the inference that the purchase of an enterprise security, unless it is based upon a forecast of a long term increase in earning power, and a relatively rapid increase at that, or unless it possesses other compensating features, is an unintelligent purchase.

That, indeed, will be our viewpoint. No other viewpoint fits in with our conception of business enterprise, or with our definition of the ideal enterprise security. No other viewpoint fits in with common sense.

When we refer to the forecast of an increase in earning power, we of course have in mind that portion of the earnings which are available for the class of securities that we are here considering—common stocks. Then:

Other things being equal, a forecast of an increase in a given corporation's earning power must be conditioned upon a forecast of an increase in gross income.

There are many, many occasions when other things are not equal. They will receive attention in due course. Let us waive them for the moment.

The gross income of a going concern derives chiefly from that concern's operations, and, in the average case, to only a minor degree from other sources, such as investments, etc.

Gross operating income is the product of the volume of goods or services sold, by selling price.

A forecast of a long term increase in gross, therefore, implies a forecast of an increase in:

1. Volume, or
2. Price, or
3. Both.

Once more assuming all other things to be equal, a given business concern usually achieves an increase in the volume of goods or services that it offers for sale by one or several of the following named routes:

a. It may, and should, become the automatic beneficiary of the increase in population.

Theoretically, at least, even a concern managed with mediocrity should sell more product, over a period of time, as the number of births in, and immigrations into, its territory exceeds the number of deaths and emigrations. The rapidity of growth on this account is obviously conditioned upon the rate of growth of potential customers in the trading territory. We may say then, that for a concern that is managed with nothing worse than

[53]

commonplace ability, and one which is not operating in a decadent industry, a forecast of an increase in the population of a given trading territory constitutes a forecast of an increase in volume.

b. By the same token, a forecast of a given concern's ability to increase the size of its trading territory, geographically, would constitute a forecast of an increase in volume.

c. Volume may be increased at the expense of competitors, either in an old trading territory or as one steps into a new territory. (With *A* and *B* generating virtually the same type of product, *A* may gain consumer preference for his own, either because of its actual superiority, or because of his ability to convince consumers of an alleged superiority.)

d. The concern with average management or better will increase its volume as the product of its industry gains in general consumer preference. (Assume that only the automobile companies with average management or better have survived the struggle; the majority of them are selling, individually, more car units today than they were fifteen years ago, when the aggregate demand for automobiles was much less insistent.)

e. A given concern stands the chance to gain in volume as the industry in which it operates gains at the expense of some other industry. (The movies have gained at the expense of the ligitimate stage; the volume of beauty parlor services at the expense of hairpins; silk and rayon knitted goods at the expense of cotton goods, etc.)

f. Volume normally increases as additional products are added to the line that a given concern has to sell.

g. Volume correspondingly increases as *new* products are developed and added.

The whole problem is summed up in the crude but expressive commercialism which refers to "selling the goods." Jones increases the volume of his sales by the simple expedient of selling more goods. Faith that he will do so, however, should be based upon economic analysis rather than upon surmise.

It will be found by actual test in a considerable number of cases that if a forecast of increase in volume cannot be predicated upon one or more of the preceding points, it cannot be predicated upon much of anything else that is tangible or believable.

Also, despite the many qualifications and exceptions which must later be made, it will be found that *more often than not,* the securities of a business concern which does not promise to increase its volume over a period of time, somewhat steadily and somewhat rapidly, are *not* desirable securities for enterprise purposes.

This increase will of course be subject to interruptions, both minor and cyclical. That is to be expected, is to be allowed for in all careful calculations, and to some extent at least can be covered by what we may call "investment policy insurance." This varying degree of fluctuation in the growth of volume is a normality, rather than an abnormality. The straight line growth in volume, over a long period of years, is a characteristic of the ideal enterprise security, rather than of the actual one. *But:*

The most satisfactory compromise with the unattainable ideal will obviously be upon those types of securities which promise to register the most infrequent temporary interruptions and the most shallow cyclical down swings, in volume growth; also upon those which, in the pitch of their long term volume growth line, promise a degree of incline more steep than the average. (Over the past three decades, the average annual growth in the physical volume of this country's industrial product has amounted to about 3½ per cent.)

COMMODITY PRICES

At the beginning of the present century various American industrial leaders were suffering from a return epidemic of a world-old and quite serious economic plague: the price-fixing complex. The "right" price was deemed to be the price that yielded the largest net profit. It was assumed that this right price was a matter over which the managers of large scale business enterprise had control; it was assumed that this control could be consistently maintained. Mr. Rockefeller could say: "You will pay 15¢ a gallon for kerosine or get none," and Mr. McCormick could issue an equally effective mandate relative to binding twine.

The system worked splendidly—for a time. It assumed (rightly, in certain conspicuous cases) that volume would be continuously under control, but it neglected to take into consideration that the public which was paying the bills was an alert and even a somewhat enlightened public, and that its political demagogues were anything but fools.

It is the major function of a monopoly to increase gross and net income through the control of prices. Monopoly was never as effective an instrument in this country as one might infer from a reading of the political literature of the first eight to ten years of the twentieth century. It was, however, more effective two and a half decades ago than it is at the present time. Hence:

The investor who counts upon monopoly to maintain the price of a given product or who counts upon any other artificial means of price maintenance, is rigging up for himself a program of the most hazardous sort, subject to cancellation without notice.

The long term trend of prices, which appears to be downward as the world's store of technological knowledge, its production capacity, and its transportation facilities increase, is decidedly against price maintenance in any given department.

Therefore, an enterprise security which *approaches* the ideal in its commodity price aspects is one which:

1. Promises not to be affected by the long term decline in commodity prices any more than the average, and preferably not so much as the average;

2. Is subject to fewer minor fluctuations than the average;

3. Suffers less violently than the average in cyclical movements of prices;

4. Is more susceptible to domestic than to world wide commodity price movements; and, finally,

5. Is not subjected to those intra-cyclical movements which have been so disturbing in particular industries in the past two decades.

Broadly speaking, those are the factors which affect selling prices most decisively:

a. Proximity of ultimate selling price to raw material price. (Raw material quotations notoriously fluctuate more violently than do so-called retail prices. The more labor that goes into a product after it leaves the raw material stage, the less violent, ordinarily, are the fluctuations in ultimate prices.)

b. The products of agriculture appear to fluctuate more widely than any other single class of commodities, and therefore the prices of goods not far removed from agricultural primary markets are obviously insecure and least subject to adequate control.

c. Prices of goods that are fixed in world markets appear to move over a wider range than prices that are made in our domestic markets.

d. Conditions of competition constitute one of the most vital forces in the intra-cyclical movements of commodity prices, as also in the major cyclical movements.

e. The workings of the old and much high-hatted law of supply and demand upon prices is so generally recognized that it need be referred to only in passing.

The corporation behind the ideal enterprise security would at the very worst be able to maintain its prices on an even keel, and at best would be able consistently to raise such prices to successively higher levels as time went on, thus adding the increased price factor to the increased volume factor, and therewith making for maximum acceleration in the growth of gross operating income.

Practically, it turns out that at best an actual corporation is fortunate if it is able to maintain its prices on a *relatively* even keel over a period of time; if it does not suffer more than the average in periods of cyclical falling prices, and if it is able to participate as much as, or more than, the average in periods of cyclical or intra-cyclical price rises, if any.

Few investors realize how many industrial fortunes are made or lost by the change of a few cents in commodity prices. Still fewer realize the utter helplessness of certain lines of industry in the face of changing raw material prices, or the independence of others which have placed themselves farther and farther away from this disrupting force.

The selling price of the product is an element of transcending importance in long term investment policy. Sometimes it becomes more significant than the trend of volume or the control of costs.

No long term investment can possibly be entered into in a careful, intelligent fashion unless the action that is taken has been preceded by as careful a calculation of long term price probabilities as is possible. Nor can any short term program be launched, intelligently, without a calculation of corresponding import.

This is a principle that is easily laid down and, seemingly, still easier to ignore—hence ignored much more often than not.

Basic lines of American industry the selling prices of which are *most* vigorously affected by fluctuations in the prices of raw materials:

Apparel
Automobile tires, rubber goods, etc.
Building materials and supplies
Chemical (especially the heavy chemicals)
Coal and coke
Copper and brass
Cotton goods
Fertilizers
Lead and zinc
Leather
Meat packing
Miscellaneous mining and smelting
Oil producing and refining
Railroad equipment
Silk goods
Steel and iron
Sugar producing and refining
Woolen goods

Basic lines of American industry the selling prices of which are *least* affected by raw material fluctuations:

Advertising, printing and publishing
Agricultural machinery
Aircraft
Automobiles
Automobile parts and accessories
Electrical equipment
Food products (other than meat)
Household products and supplies
Shoes
Machinery and machine equipment
Drugs, medicines, cosmetics, etc.
Miscellaneous manufacturing
Miscellaneous service
Office and business equipment
Paper and paper products

[61]

Radio, phonograph and musical instruments
Railroads
Rayon
Retail trade
Shipping and shipbuilding
Theatres, motion pictures and amusements
Tobacco and tobacco products
Public utilities

Basic lines of American industry in which competitive conditions have in recent years had the *most* depressing effects upon prices:

Aircraft
Apparel
Automobiles
Automobile parts and accessories
Automobile tires, rubber goods, etc.
Building materials and supplies
Coal and coke
Copper and brass
Cotton goods
Fertilizers
Leather
Oil producing and refining
Paper and paper products
Radio, phonograph and musical instruments
Railroad equipment
Rayon
Retail trade
Shipping and shipbuilding
Silk goods
Steel and iron
Woolen goods

Basic lines of American industry in which competitive conditions have in recent years had the *least* depressing effect upon selling prices:

Advertising, printing and publishing
Agricultural machinery
Chemicals (industrials)

[62]

Electrical equipment
Food products (other than meat)
Household products and supplies
Lead and zinc
Shoes
Machinery and machine equipment
Meat packing
Miscellaneous mining and smelting
Drugs, medicines, cosmetics, etc.
Miscellaneous manufacturing
Miscellaneous service
Office and business equipment
Railroads
Sugar refining
Theatres, motion pictures and amusements
Tobacco and tobacco products
Public utilities

To sum up, the ideal enterprise security is the one promising the maximum amount of growth in disbursable profits, and promising to maintain this rate of growth *ad infinitum*.

Disbursable income is net income.

Net is a derivative of gross; it is what remains of gross after costs and service on senior securities have been paid. It therefore must inevitably bear a direct relationship to gross.

Actual security market operations are compromises with the ideal. The purchase or maintenance of an interest in a business concern which does not hold the promise of materially expanding its gross revenue over a period of time, becomes, if judged by these standards, a dubious compromise. The least that can be said is that such an operation, unless there are compensating features of a very exceptional

[63]

sort, throws the burden of proof as to its validity upon the operator himself rather than upon the market.

Stated still more bluntly, we here venture the opinion that the assumption or maintenance of a long term enterprise position in the security of a corporation which does not promise materially to increase its gross income over a period of time is more often than not unjustified—even dangerous.

The fact that a statistical record of gross over a past period is so frequently unobtainable does not, unfortunately, relieve the conservative investor of the necessity for a careful forecast before he takes a decisive action, and the necessity for continuous reforecast after he has acted.

When the exact figures upon which to base a statistical forecast are not to be had, the indirect method of projecting future probabilities becomes the only feasible one. Gross in this case is an unknown quantity; volume, under such circumstances, is usually also unknown. Knowledge as to price varies radically from one industry to another. The whole study becomes nebulous, inexact, confused.

But it cannot be side-stepped—that is, not if one is really striving to invest carefully, rather than merely to act on the basis of guess. Some forecast, at least as to the *direction* and *general trend* of gross, must be made. It must be the best forecast that it is possible to make. Out of the nebulous and inexact there must come concrete ideas, ideas based upon sufficient research and analysis to render them reasonably trustworthy.

To repeat, even at the risk of tedium: the forecast as to the trend of gross income, over a period of time, is an absolutely essential element in any carefully planned security market action.

About one-half of the largest corporations, the stocks of which are actively traded in on the leading exchanges, make public any statistical record whatsoever as to their gross income. Taking all stocks listed on all organized exchanges throughout the country, the fraction becomes much smaller, possibly dropping as low as one-fourth or one-fifth.

Naturally, in a financial community composed of such complacent and obliging investors as in America, it would be preposterous to assume that any considerable number of them would actually demand more information relative to gross income than they are now receiving. It would be preposterous to assume that those who are supplying the money to finance business would go so far as to demand that they be provided with adequate tools for determining whether they are justified in assuming the risk in the original instance, or in continuing to carry the risk.

This would be quite too much.

But it should do no harm to point out that, if the average American investor's interest in basic value ever came to exceed his interest in price, the component factors that go to make up value would begin to receive more attention. Gross income is one of these component factors of value.

It should also do no harm to point out that if the owners of American industry really expressed a desire, insistently and over a period of time, for a continuous statistical record of gross income in the numerous cases where such data are now withheld, their plea might not always be denied.

The Standard Statistics Company recently completed a careful comparative study of the income accounts of nearly six hundred leading American industrial concerns, the stocks of which are actively traded in on the New York Stock Exchange and other leading outside exchanges. The following tabulation lists those which did, and those which did not, report gross income in 1929:

Reported Gross Income in 1929	*Did Not Report Gross Income in* 1929
Abraham & Straus	
Adams-Millis Corp.	Abitibi Power and Paper Co.
Advance Rumely Co.	Air-Way Electric Appliance Corp.
Air Reduction Co.	Ajax Rubber Co.
Allis Chalmers Manufacturing Co.	Allied Chemical and Dye Corp.
Alpha Portland Cement Co.	Aluminum Co. of America

Reported Gross Income in 1929

Amerada Corp.
American Bosch Magneto Corp.
American Encaustic Tiling Co.
American-Hawaiian Steamship Co.
American Ice Co.
American Machine and Foundry
American Radiator and Standard Sanitary
American Republics Corp.
American Rolling Mill Co.
American Seating Co.
American Solvents and Chemical Corp.
American Stores Co.
American Type Founders Co.
American Writing Paper Co.
Anaconda Copper Mining Co.
Arlington Mills
Arnold Constable Corp.
Art Metal Construction Co.
Associated Apparel Industries
Atlantic, Gulf and West Indies S. S. Lines
Atlantic Refining Co.
Atlas Plywood Corp.
Atlas Powder
Atlas Tack Corp.
Auburn Auto Co.
Baldwin Locomotive Works
Barnsdall Corp.
Beatrice Creamery Co.
Beech-Nut Packing Co.
Best & Co.
Bethlehem Steel Corp.
Bigelow-Sanford Carpet Co.
Bloomingdale Bros.
Blumenthal (Sidney) & Co.
Borden Co.
Brach (E. J.) & Sons
Brockway Motor Truck
Brown Shoe
Brunswick-Balke-Collender Co.
Bucyrus Erie Co.

Did Not Report Gross Income in 1929

Amalgamated Leather Cos.
American Agricultural Chemical
American Bank Note Co.
American Beet Sugar Co.
American Brake Shoe and Foundry Co.
American Brown Boveri Electric Corp.
American Can Co.
American Car and Foundry Co.
American Chain Co.
American Chicle
American Cyanamid Co.
American Home Products Corp.
American Locomotive Co.
American Metal Co.
American Safety Razor Corp.
American Ship Building Co.
American Ship and Commerce Corp.
American Smelting and Refining Co.
American Snuff Co.
American Steel Foundries
American Sugar Refining Co.
American Sumatra Tobacco
American Tobacco Co.
American Woolen Co.
American Zinc, Lead and Smelting
Anaconda Wire Cable Co.
Anchor Cap Corp.
Apponaug Co.
Archer-Daniels Midland
Armour & Co. (Ill.)
Artloom Corp.
Associated Dry Goods Corp.
Babcock & Wilcox Co.
Barnet Leather Co.
Bayuk Cigars
Belding Heminway Co.
Bliss (E. W.) Co.
Bohn Aluminum and Brass Corp.
Bon Ami Co.

[67]

Reported Gross Income in 1929

Bunker Hill & Sullivan Min. & Con. Co.
Burns Bros. (N. J.)
Burroughs Adding Machine Co.
Butterick Co.
Byers (A. M.) Co.
Calumet and Arizona Mining Co.
Calumet and Hecla Consol. Copper
Cannon Mills Co.
Caterpillar Trac. Co.
Cavanagh-Dobbs
Celotex Co.
Central Aguirre Associates
Century Ribbon Mills
Cerro de Pasco Copper Corp.
Childs Co.
Chrysler Corp.
City Ice and Fuel Co.
Cluett-Peabody
Coca-Cola Co.
Colgate-Palmolive Peet Co.
Columbian Carbon Co.
Conde Nast Publications
Congress Cigar Co.
Consolidated Film Industries
Consolidated Laundries Corp.
Consolidated Mining and Smelting Co.
Consolidated Textile Corp.
Continental Oil Co. (Del.)
Cosden Oil Co.
Crosley Radio Corp.
Cuban-American Sugar Co.
Cuban Dominican Sugar Corp.
Cudahy Packing Co.
Curtis Publishing Co.
Cutler-Hammer
Devoe & Raynolds
Dome Mines
Dominion Stores
Dominion Textile Co.
Dubilier Condenser Corp.
Durham Hosiery Mills
Eastern Steamship Lines

Did Not Report Gross Income in 1929

Borg-Warner Corp.
Botany Consolidated Mills
Briggs Manufacturing Co.
Briggs & Stratton Corp.
Brunswick Terminal and Railway Securities Co.
Budd (Edw. G.) Manufacturing Co.
Budd Wheel Co.
Bush Terminal Co.
Butler Bros.
Butte Copper and Zinc Co.
California Packing Corp.
Campbell, Wyant & Cannon Fdry.
Canadian Bronze Co.
Canadian Power and Paper Corp.
Case (J. I.) Co.
Castle (A. M.) & Co.
Celanese Corp. of America
Certain-teed Products Corp.
Chicago Pneumatic Tool Co.
Cleveland Worsted Mills
Cockshutt Plow Co.
Cohn-Hall-Marx
Collins & Aikman Corp.
Colorado Fuel and Iron Co.
Commercial Solvents Corp.
Compania Swift Internacional S. A. C.
Congoleum-Nairn
Consolidated Cigar Corp.
Container Corp. of America
Continental Baking Corp.
Continental Can Co.
Continental Motors Corp.
Corn Products Refining Co.
Coty
Crex Carpet Co.
Crucible Steel Co. of America
Cuba Cane Sugar
Cuneo Press

Reported Gross Income in 1929	*Did Not Report Gross Income in* 1929
Electric Storage Battery Co.	
Elk Horn Coal Corp.	Decker (Alfred) & Cohn
Endicott-Johnson Corp.	Deere & Co.
Equitable Office Bldg. Corp.	Diamond Match Co.
Eureka Vacuum Cleaner Co.	Drug, Inc.
Fair (The)	duPont (E. I.) de Nemours & Co.
Fairbanks, Morse & Co.	Eastman Kodak Co. of N. J.
Fajardo Sugar Co. of Porto Rico	Eaton Axle & Spring Co.
Federal Mining and Smelting Co.	Electric Auto-Lite Co.
Federated Metals Corp.	Electric Boat Co.
Firestone Tire and Rubber Co.	Evans Auto Loading Co.
First National Stores	Evans-Wallower Lead Co.
Fisk Rubber Co.	Federal Motor Truck
Follansbee Bros. Co.	Florsheim Shoe Co.
Formica Insulation Co.	Ford Motor Co. of Canada
Foundation Co.	Foster Wheeler Corp.
Fox Film Corp.	Franklin (H. H.) Mfg. Co.
Freeport Texas Co.	Fraser Cos.
Gardner Motors Co.	Gabriel Co.
General American Tank Car	General Baking Corp.
General Asphalt Co.	General Cable Corp.
General Bronze Corp.	General Railway Signal Co.
General Cigar	General Refractories Co.
General Electric Co.	Gillette Safety Razor Co.
General Fireproofing Co.	Godchaux Sugars
General Foods Corp.	Gold Dust Corp.
General Motors Corp.	Gotham Silk Hosiery
General Outdoor Advertsing Co.	Great Western Sugar Co.
General Tire and Rubber Co.	Harbison-Walker Refractories Co.
Gimbel Bros.	Hart, Schaffner & Marx
Gleaner Combine Harvester Corp.	Helme (George W.) Co.
Glidden Co.	Illinois Brick Co.
Gobel (Adolf)	Illinois Pacific Glass Corp.
Goodrich (B.F.) Co.	Imperial Oil Co.
Goodyear Tire and Rubber Co.	Industrial Rayon Corp.
Graham-Paige Motors Corp.	Ingersoll-Rand Co.
Granby Cons. Mining, Smelting and Power Co.	Intercontinental Rubber Co.
Grand (F. W.)-Silver Stores	International Agricultural Chemical
Grand Union Co.	
Grant (W. T.) & Co.	International Business Machines Corp.
Guantanamo Sugar Co.	
Gulf Oil Corp. of Pennsylvania	International Combustion Engineering
Gulf States Steel Co.	

Reported Gross Income in 1929

Hahn Department Stores
Hart-Carter Co.
Hayes Body Corp.
Hazeltine Corp.
Hecla Mining Co.
Hercules Powder Co.
Hershey Chocolate Corp.
Hires (Chas. E.)
Holland Furnace Co.
Hollander (A.) & Son
Hollinger Consol. Gold Mines
Hormel (Geo. A.) & Co.
Houston Oil Co. of Texas
Howe Sound Co.
Hudson Motor Car
Humble Oil and Refining Co.
Hupp Motor Car Corp.
Independent Oil and Gas Co.
Indian Refining Co.
Inland Steel Co.
Inspiration Consol. Copper Co.
International Cement Corp.
International Mercantile Marine Co.
International Printing Ink Corp.
International Shoe Co.
International Silver Co.
Interstate Department Stores
Jewel Tea Co.
Johns-Manville Corp.
Jordan Motor Car
Kaufmann Dept. Stores
Kayser (Julius) & Co.
Kelvinator Corp.
Keystone Steel & Wire Co.
Kimberly-Clark Corp.
Kinney (G. R.) Co.
Kresge (S. S.)
Kresge Dept. Stores
Kress (S. H.) & Co.
Kroger Grocery and Baking Co.
Lee Rubber and Tire Corp.
Lehigh Coal and Navigation Co.
Lehigh Portland Cement Co.

Did Not Report Gross Income in 1929

International Harvester Co.
International Nickel Co. of Canada
International Salt Co. of New Jersey
Intertype Corp.
Island Creek Coal Co.
Jones & Laughlin Steel Corp.
Kelly-Springfield Tire Co.
Kelsey-Hayes Wheel Corp.
Kennecott Copper
Kuppenheimer (B.) & Co.
Lambert Co.
Lehn & Fink Products Co.
Libby, McNeill & Libby
Libby-Owens-Ford Glass Co.
Liggett & Myers Tobacco Co.
Lima Locomotive Works
Long-Bell Lumber Corp.
Loose-Wiles Biscuit Co.
Lorillard (P.) Co.
McIntyre Porcupine Mines
Mallinson (H. R.) & Co.
Manhattan Shirt
Marion Steam Shovel Co.
Marlin-Rockwell Corp.
Massey Harris Co.
Mathieson Alkali Works
Mergenthaler Linotype Co.
Mid-Continent Petroleum Corp.
Midland Steel Products
Morris (Philip) & Co.
Motor Products Corp.
Motor Wheel Corp.
Mullins Manufacturing
Murray Corp. of America
Nashawena Mills
Nash Motors
National Acme Co.
National Biscuit Co.
National Lead Co.
National Radiator Corp.
National Rubber Machine Co.

Reported Gross Income in 1929	*Did Not Report Gross Income in* 1929
Lehigh Valley Coal Corp.	
Link Belt Co.	National Sugar Refining Co. of
Liquid Carbonic Corp.	N. J.
Loew's, Inc.	National Supply Co. (of Del.)
Ludlum Steel Co.	Newton Steel Co.
MacAndrews & Forbes	New York Air Brake Co.
Mack Trucks	Niles-Bement-Pond Co.
Macy (R. H.) & Co.	Nipissing Mines Co.
Magma Copper Corp.	North American Car Corp.
Manati Sugar Co.	Northwest Engineering Co.
Manhattan Electrical Supply Co.	Norwalk Tire and Rubber
Marmon Motor Car	Ohio Oil Co.
Martin-Parry Corp.	Otis Elevator Co.
May Dept. Stores Co.	Otis Steel Co.
Maytag Co.	Pan American Petroleum and
McCall Corp.	Transport Co.
McCrory Stores Corp.	Paramount Publix Corp.
McGraw-Hill Publishing Co.	Parke, Davis & Co.
McKeesport Tin Plate Co.	Park-Utah Cons. Mines
McKesson & Robbins (Md.)	Penick & Ford
Melville Shoe Corp.	Phoenix Hosiery Co.
Mengel Co.	Pillsbury Flour Mills
Miami Copper Co.	Pitney Bowes Postage Meter Co.
Miller (I.) & Sons	Porto Rican-American Tobacco Co.
Minneapolis-Honeywell Regulator	Pressed Steel Car Co.
Co.	Price Bros. & Co.
Minneapolis-Moline Power Imple-	Pullman
ment Co.	Quaker Oats Co.
Mohawk Carpet Mills	Real Silk Hosiery Mills
Mohawk Rubber Co.	Reis (Robert) & Co.
Montgomery Ward & Co.	Revere Copper and Brass
Moon Motor Car	Reynolds (R. J.) Tobacco Co.
Moto Meter Gauge and Equip-	Richman Bros. Co.
ment Co.	Ross Gear and Tool Co.
Munsingwear	Royal Typewriter Co.
National Bellas Hess Co.	St. Joseph Lead Co.
National Cash Register Co.	Savage Arms Corp.
National Dairy Products	Schulte Retail Stores
National Department Stores	Seeman Bros.
National Distillers Products Corp.	Shubert Theatre Corp.
National Enameling and Stamping	Shell Union Oil Corp.
Co.	Simms Petroleum
National Tea Co.	Sloss-Sheffield Steel and Iron Co.
National Trade Journals	Smith (A. O.) Corp.

[71]

Reported Gross Income in 1929

Naumkeag Steam Cotton Co.
Nevada Consolidated Copper Co.
Newberry (J. J.) Co.
Newport Co.
New York Dock Co.
Noranda Mines
Oil Well Supply Co.
Oliver Farm Equipment Co.
Oppenheim Collins
Pacific Mills
Packard Motor Car
Park & Tilford
Pathe Exchange
Patino Mines and Enterprises Consol.
Peerless Motor Car
Penn-Dixie Cement Corp.
Pennsylvania Coal and Coke Corp.
Pepperell Manufacturing
Phelphs-Dodge Co.
Philadelphia & Reading Coal and Iron Corp.
Phillips-Jones Corp.
Phillips Petroleum Co.
Pittsburgh Coal Co.
Pittsburgh Terminal Coal Corp.
Polymet Mfg. Corp.
Poor & Co.
Powdrell & Alexander
Prairie Oil and Gas Co.
Prairie Pipe Line
Procter & Gamble
Producers and Refiners Corp.
Punta Alegre Sugar
Pure Oil Co.
Purity Bakeries Corp.
Radio Corp. of America
R.-K.-O. Corp.
Raybestos-Manhattan
Remington Arms Co.
Remington-Rand
Reo Motor Car Co.
Reynolds Metals
Richfield Oil Co. (Calif.)

Did Not Report Gross Income in 1929

Spicer Manufacturing Corp.
Standard Oil Co. of California
Standard Oil Co. of Indiana
Standard Oil Co. of Kentucky
Standard Oil Co. of New Jersey
Standard Oil Co. of New York
Standard Plate Glass Co.
Stewart-Warner Corp.
Stromberg-Carlson Telephone Manufacturing Co.
Stroock (S.) & Co.
Swift & Co.
Symington Co.
Texas Corp.
Thompson Products
Timken-Detroit Axle Co.
Timken Roller Bearing Co.
Todd Shipyards Corp.
Transue & Williams Steel Forging Corp.
Trico Products Corp.
Underwood-Elliott-Fisher Co.
Union Bag and Paper Corp.
Union Carbide and Carbon Corp.
Union Tank Car Co.
United Electric Coal Cos.
United Fruit Co.
United Piece Dye Works
United Shoe Machinery Corp.
U. S. Gypsum Co.
U. S. Hoffman Machinery Corp.
U. S. Industrial Alcohol Co.
U. S. Leather Co.
U. S. Pipe and Foundry Co.
U. S. Smelting, Refining and Mining
United States Tobacco Co.
Universal Pipe and Radiator Co.
Vacuum Oil Co.
Vanadium Corp. of America
Van Raalte Co.
Virginia-Carolina Chemical Corp.
Walworth Co.

Reported Gross Income in 1929	*Did Not Report Gross Income in* 1929
Rio Grande Oil Co. of Delaware	
Safeway Stores	Ward Baking Corp.
Scott Paper Co.	Warner Bros. Pictures
Seagrave Corp.	Webster-Eisenlohr
Sears, Roebuck & Co.	Wesson Oil and Snowdrift
Seiberling Rubber Co.	Westinghouse Air Brake Co.
Servel	Weston Electrical Instrument Corp.
Shattuck (F. G.) Co.	
Sherwin-Williams Co.	White Sewing Machine Corp.
Simmons Co.	White Star Refining Co.
Sinclair Cons. Oil Corp.	Wilcox-Rich Corp.
Skelly Oil Co.	Wilson & Co.
Snider Packing Corp.	Worthington Pump and Machine Corp.
Southern Dairies	
South Porto Rico Sugar	Young (L. A.) Spring and Wire Corp.
Spiegel, May, Stern Co.	
Standard Commercial Tobacco Co.	Youngstown Sheet and Tube Co.
Standard Oil Co. of Kansas	
Standard Oil Co. of Ohio	
Standard Textile Products Co.	
Studebaker Corp.	
Submarine Boat Corp.	
Sun Oil Co.	
Super Maid Corp.	
Superior Steel Corp.	
Sweets Co. of America	
Teck-Hughes Gold Mines	
Telautograph Corp.	
Tennessee Copper and Chemical Corp.	
Texas Gulf Sulphur Co.	
Thatcher Manufacturing Co.	
Tide Water Associated Oil Co.	
Transcontinental Oil Co.	
Trans-Lux Daylight Pict. Screen Corp.	
Truscon Steel Co.	
Union Oil Co. of California	
United Biscuit Co. of America	
United Business Publishers	
United Carbon Co.	
United Cigar Stores Co. of America	
United Engineering and Foundry Co.	

Reported Gross Income in 1929	*Did Not Report Gross Income in* 1929
U. S. Dairy Products Corp.	
U. S. Distributing Corp.	
U. S. Finishing Co.	
U. S. Freight Co.	
U. S. Rubber Co.	
U. S. Steel Corp.	
United Verde Extension Mining Co.	
Universal Leaf Tobacco	
Universal Pictures Co.	
Vadsco Sales Corp.	
Vulcan Detinning Co.	
Wahl Co.	
Warner-Quinlan Co.	
Warren Brothers Co.	
Warren Foundry and Pipe Co.	
Western Dairy Products	
Westinghouse Electric and Manufacturing Co.	
Westvaco Chlorine Products Corp.	
White Motor Co.	
White Rock Mineral Springs Co.	
Williams Oil-O-Matic Heating Corp.	
Willys Overland Co.	
Woolworth (F. W.)	
Wrigley (Wm.), Jr., Co.	
Yale & Towne Mfg. Co.	
Yellow Truck and Coach	

3. THE YAWNING GAPS BETWEEN GROSS AND NET

One of the most vital problems of the investor in enterprise securities is to formulate, in advance, a reasonably accurate estimate of the income that will be available, over a period of time, for the security which he holds.

We know that this estimate of future probabilities, so long as it is made by human beings, can never be an exact one. But at the same time we know that the problem is not unyielding to careful study. Hence we know that a carefully studied estimate, built with all the tools of research, analysis, and statistics that the investor can command, must be better than blind guess. And from there it is only one more step to the principle that the results achieved in investment enterprise must, over a period of time, bear a direct relationship to the investor's skill in estimating income trends.

It is going rather far to assert (as sometimes is asserted) that if the investor's estimate of value is reasonably accurate, he need have no concern with price—price should take care of itself.

Price *should* take care of itself in the expression of real value, *and does so more often than not.* But not always, unhappily. Now and again it becomes a thing so remote from the value which it is reflecting that the relationship can hardly be identified. But it is *not* going too far to say that an important degree of relationship between value and price *must always exist*, and therefore that the problem is considerably more than half solved when the value riddle has been figured.

Net income, as was earlier pointed out, is a derivative of gross. It was suggested than an estimate of net logically starts with an estimate of gross.

It starts there—but only starts. Between gross and net there are a series of yawning gaps into which various fractions of gross income fall and disappear on the way down to net. Here it will be to our purpose to deal only with the most important of these and, moreover, to deal with them in a quite perfunctory fashion. The more detailed treatment (which assuredly is justified from the standpoint of the development of sound investment practice) lies without the scope of this particular study. Our immediate objective will be served if we are able only to suggest that these yawning gaps between gross income on the one hand, and net income available for the common stock on the other hand, *are* elements of no small concern to the conservative investor, and that the more weight

[76]

he gives them in his analysis, the more secure that analysis is likely to be.

The gaps which yawn the most hungrily for their respective fractions of gross income are:

Costs of production and sales.

Reserves for depreciation, depletion, obsolescence, and other purposes.

Fixed charges and preferred dividends.

Uniformly it should be the conservative investor's objective to explain short term variations in these important items, and to detect in advance longer term changes. It is the element of eternal change that is the most vital in the determination of the going value of a business enterprise. Favorable changes are those which enlarge disbursable income; unfavorable changes those which diminish it. All security forecast is therefore, in one sense at least, the estimate of impending change.

Costs

Costs, on the average, consume the major portion of gross income. (It is seldom that a business enterprise is able to save as much as 50 per cent of gross for net; in the rare cases where it is able to do so, the phenomenon is usually of very short term duration. In the long run, competition will adequately take care of such abnormally fortunate situations.)

[77]

The component elements that go to make up costs, in business enterprise in the aggregate, are so infinitely varied that it would be futile to attempt to examine even the most important of them in anything like comprehensive detail. The shifting prices paid for raw materials; the prices paid for services (labor and management); the costs of making an X volume of sales, an XY volume, and an XYZ volume; the cost of production by process A, by process AB, and by process ABC; the cost of changing from Process A to Process AB, and still later from AB to ABC; costs of renewals; costs of extensions; costs of developing and marketing new products; costs incurred by abnormal competitive conditions—these better known kinds of costs are a mere handful of names when compared with the total of all such elements.

Rather than attempt any sort of an analysis of the determinants of enterprise costs, we shall here merely call attention to some of the more important investment principles which revolve about costs, and which the investor should constantly be on the alert to detect.

I. It is not necessarily a sign of unfavorable change if costs rise, relatively, more rapidly than gross income, although the development of such a situation more often than not furnishes the occasion for grave suspicion.

[78]

To avoid unnecessary complications in the examples immediately following, we will assume that the hypothetical corporations to be noted have but one class of security outstanding, common stock, and that *all* of the gaps between gross and net available for the common are accounted for in the single item "costs," as the term is here used.

Corporation *A* does a gross business of $10,000,-000 in 1930, at a cost of $9,000,000: By 1935, gross has increased 50 per cent, while costs have increased 51 per cent. The comparative income account, skeletonized, would read:

Date	Gross income	Costs	Net for common	Per cent increase in net
1930	$10,000,000	$ 9,000,000	$1,000,000	
1935	15,000,000	13,590,000	1,410,000	+41

But observe that any program in which the rate of cost increase outstrips the rate of gross increase has its obvious limitations.

Corporation *B*, having increased its gross 50 per cent by 1935 and its costs 55 per cent:

Date	Gross income	Costs	Net for common	Per cent increase in net
1930	$10,000,000	$ 9,000,000	$1,000,000	
1935	15,000,000	13,950,000	1,050,000	+5

Corporation *C*, having increased its gross 50 per cent by 1935 and its costs 60 per cent:

[79]

Date	Gross income	Costs	Net for common	Per cent decrease in net
1930	$10,000,000	$ 9,000,000	$1,000,000	
1935	15,000,000	14,400,000	600,000	−40

II. Other things being equal, the corporation which can hold the rate of its cost increase to an equivalent with that of its gross increase is more favorably situated than the one which must permit a relative greater increase in costs than in gross.

Corporation *D*, having increased both its gross income and its costs 50 per cent by 1935:

Date	Gross income	Costs	Net for common	Per cent increase in net
1930	$10,000,000	$ 9,000,000	$1,000,000	
1935	15,000,000	13,500,000	1,500,000	+50

III. Still more favorably situated is the corporation which is able to decrease its costs, relatively, as gross income expands.

Corporation *E*, having increased its gross 50 per cent by 1935 but having increased its costs only 49 per cent:

Date	Gross income	Costs	Net for common	Per cent increase in net
1930	$10,000,000	$ 9,000,000	$1,000,000	
1935	15,000,000	13,410,000	1,590,000	+59

Note the amazing rapidity with which net available for the common stock rises if costs can be stepped down even moderately.

Corporation *F*, having increased its gross 50 per cent by 1935 but having increased its costs only 45 per cent:

Date	Gross income	Costs	Net for common	Per cent increase in net
1930	$10,000,000	$ 9,000,000	$1,000,000	
1935	15,000,000	13,050,000	1,950,000	+95

These are first reader principles to the truck man, the delicatessen keeper, the dentist, the lawyer, the industrial magnates who are responsible for the operating results of the biggest corporations. They all want to increase the volume and (or) prices of goods or services sold, and therewith to increase gross income. They want to achieve this enhancement of gross on a scale of constantly diminishing aggregate cost, if possible, or, at worst, on a cost scale that does not rise, relatively, with greater rapidity than gross.

It is this purpose which is behind the constant competitive struggle for greater volume, new markets, etc. All business is conscious of this underlying motivating force—is constantly wrestling with it.

Seldom can the trend of costs be estimated in other than a general way by the average investor. Naturally, and quite reasonably, corporations make public, in this respect, as little information as possible. Where gross income is reported, a close approximation can be arrived at. Where there is no gross income report, only the broadest generalization is feasible.

In the 1921–1929 bull market, few points excited the speculative imagination more than published reports that this or that corporation had developed new technological processes which would work out in a net reduction of costs. New methods for rolling sheet steel and for making seamless pipe; Duco as a substitute for the old style automobile enamel; new machines for cigarette making; new processes for coloring motion picture films; an infinite number of new chemical processes; new combustion processes—these were only a few of the many developments bearing upon costs (and promising a reduction in unit costs) which were capitalized, spectacularly, in the last big bull market.

Thus costs present a real and significant element in the investor's problem. Statistics which approximately report their trend, and even the more general information which even *suggests* this trend, are valuable; a place must be made for these data in the investor's analysis. *Costs fill the largest of the several gaps between gross and net. Hence no estimate of the long term trend of net which ignores costs can be at all trustworthy.*

RESERVES

Jones is an independent truckman, operating a single vehicle "on his own." He purchases a new $2,500 truck. He is a careful business man, is Jones. He estimates that three years hence this car he has just bought will have served its term of usefulness, so far as he is concerned, and that he can then sell it for $500.

At that time he will need another car, if he is going to stay in the trucking business. If, in addition to his various operating and maintenance charges, he sets aside $55.55 each month, he will have, at the end of three years, the $2,000 in cash which, added to the $500 he will get for his old car, will enable him to purchase a new one.

This is the theory upon which business concerns operate when they set up reserves for depreciation, depletion, and obsolescence. Theoretically, such reserves are real money, set aside out of earnings each year and withheld from stock owners, and either utilized in renewals of plant and equipment, or held in abeyance pending the need for such utilization. These reserves are more or less meaningless if they represent merely bookkeeping transactions. They have considerably more significance if they are actually reflected in spendable surplus.

If Jones sets aside only $25 per month, pending the obsolescence of his truck and the purchase of a new one, he will probably be obliged to borrow some money when the renewal date arrives.

If he sets aside nothing, he will have more money for his own use as he goes along and doubtless will have more fun, but when his equipment becomes no longer economical to use, he will *certainly* be obliged to make special arrangements when the time comes for new capital outlays.

This analyst is not one who insists that a corporation cannot be conservatively operated, nor operated for the best interests of stockholders, unless large reserves for depreciation, depletion, and obsolescence are set aside each year. It might very well be conservative practice to pay out a certain portion of this reserve money to stockholders, let them have the use and enjoyment of it as they go along, and do what financing is necessary when the time for large capital outlays arrives. It might be so, and specific examples of cases in which it has been so can readily be cited— although most engineers will throw up their hands in horror at the mere mention of such an heretical program.

The more essential thing would seem to be that the stockholder, or prospective stockholder, should really have a clear understanding of his corporation's depreciation policies, whatever they may be and whatever the needs of the particular situation may demand, and to evaluate his securities on the basis of such an understanding.

Reserves for such purposes become an income account item from year to year. This item stands between gross and net. Therefore it is one of the determinants of net. Over-generous reserves or inadequate ones may easily lead to a net income figure which is deceptive.

Special reserves—for contigencies, inventory adjustments, etc.—should be regarded in the same light. First one should know whether they are real cash reserves or merely bookkeeping transactions; then one should know their purposes and the needs which occasioned them.

Fixed Charges and Preferred Dividends

A short cut to the definition of fixed charges is to say that this is the portion of costs represented by interest payments on bonds, bank loans, or other forms of formal indebtedness. On the average, the preponderant portion of fixed charges are payments of bondholders.

Preferred dividends need no explanation.

These two kinds of costs reflect different ways of raising money for necessary corporate purposes —for initial financing, for the consummation of mergers, for other types of extensions or expansion, sometimes even for renewal of obsolete equipment (as with Jones, when he failed to set aside a depreciation reserve for his slowly expiring truck). Not infrequently, also, these senior costs are in the nature of bail, with which a corporation unwillingly saddles itself—a corporation that has got itself into a hard fix, and that has to be bailed out of debtor's prison. No common stock offering could possibly be made attractive to security purchasers, under certain circumstances; securities possessing a better guarantee are the only ones that are salable.

In the matter of senior obligations generally, it is indeed difficult to lay down any comprehensive set of principles for the common stock holder's guidance. The circumstances surrounding the assumption of such obligations vary so widely from one occasion to another that rules of thumb become highly dangerous tools; what is Corporation *X's* meat and bread in one instance may very well become Corporation *Y's* poison in another.

A limited number of aspects of the situation, however, are quite clear:

I. The assumption by a corporation of a new or an additional senior security obligation as the only practical means of escape from serious financial distress may work to the benefit of the common stock holder over a period of time, in that it gives the concern a new lease on life, averts a receivership, and probably prevents the common stock from becoming valueless.

But for some time prior to this climactic action, the common stock holder's position has been steadily deteriorating; it cannot have been otherwise, else the financial climax would not have occurred. When the prior obligations are thus placed ahead of his own position, about all the common stock owner has left, for the time being, is hope. He will be well advised to use every tool of research and analysis at his command in an effort to avoid finding himself in such a situation; if he holds the position of an enterprise partner in a corporation which is sliding *toward* such a complication, to abandon that position too soon rather than too late.

II. A relatively heavy load of interest charges and preferred stock dividends ahead of a given common stock adds to the speculative hazards of that stock. Being fixed obligations, these prior charges rapidly detract from common stock values in periods of

declining earnings, but similarly help to account for rapidly changing values of common stocks, on the favorable side, in periods of rising earnings.

A few simple calculations will illustrate these points quite vividly. Let us turn back for a moment to the skeletonized income accounts of certain hypothetical corporations which were worked out in the section immediately preceding, and set up an additional series of accounts so that the $1,000,-000 which was available for the common stock holders in 1930 in all previous cases, will be in the instances we are about to consider available for *all* security owners, with $150,000 going to bond owners regularly, another $150,000 to preferred-stock holders, and only the remainder ($700,000) available for common stock holders.

Note the difference under this new set of facts.

Year	Net for all security owners	Obligatory payments on bonds and pre-ferred stocks	Net for common	Per cent change in net for common
	Corporation *A* (as shown on page 79)			
1930	$1,000,000	0	$1,000,000	
1935	1,410,000	0	1,410,000	+41.0
	Corporation *AA*			
1930	1,000,000	$300,000	700,000	
1935	1,410,000	300,000	1,110,000	58.6

Year	Net for all security owners	Obligatory payments on bonds and pre-ferred stocks	Net for common	Per cent change in net for common
Corporation *B* (as shown on page 79)				
1930	1,000,000	0	1,000,000	
1935	1,050,000	0	1,050,000	+ 5.0
Corporation *BB*				
1930	1,000,000	300,000	700,000	
1935	1,050,000	300,000	750,000	+ 7.1
Corporation *C* (as shown on page 80)				
1930	1,000,000	0	1,000,000	
1935	600,000	0	600,000	−40.0
Corporation *CC*				
1930	1,000,000	300,000	700,000	
1935	600,000	300,000	300,000	−57.1
Corporation *D* (as shown on page 80)				
1930	1,000,000	0	1,000,000	
1935	1,500,000	0	1,500,000	+50.0
Corporation *DD*				
1930	1,000,000	300,000	700,000	
1935	1,500,000	300,000	1,200,000	+71.4
Corporation *F* (as shown on page 81)				
1930	1,000,000	0	1,000,000	
1935	1,950,000	0	1,950,000	+95.0
Corporation *FF*				
1930	1,000,000	300,000	700,000	
1935	1,950,000	300,000	1,650,000	+135.7

Note what happens if we further increase the load of senior securities. Say that it is doubled, or brought up to $600,000. Look at our two most extreme cases in this circumstance:

[89]

Year	Net for all security owners	Obligatory payments on bonds and pre-ferred stocks	Net for common	Per cent change in net for common
Corporation C (as shown on page 80)				
1930	$1,000,000	0	$1,000,000	
1935	600,000	0	600,000	− 40.0
Corporation CC (as shown on			89)	
1930	1,000,000	300,000	700,000	
1935	600,000	300,000	300,000	− 57.1
Corporation CCC				
1930	1,000,000	600,000	400,000	
1935	600,000	600,000	0	−100
Corporation F (as shown on page 81)				
1930	1,000,000	0	1,000,000	
1935	1,950,000	0	1,950,000	+ 95
Corporation FF (as shown on page 89)				
1930	1,000,000	300,000	700,000	
1935	1,950,000	300,000	1,650,000	+135.7
Corporation FFF				
1930	1,000,000	600,000	400,000	
1935	1,950,000	600,000	1,350,000	+237.5

III. Hence, the heavier the load of senior securities ahead of the common, the greater are likely to be the discrepancies in the earning value of that common stock as the economic scene shifts from prosperity to depression or vice versa.

The calculations immediately preceding are by no means preposterous. At the bottom of the 1929–1931 bear market, certain large investment trusts were very nearly in the position of Corporation *CCC*. They had been lavishly weighted with preferred stocks. Along with the terrific shrinkage in their aggregate assets, their incomes had diminished so greatly that preferred dividends were only about covered. Their common stocks sold at 10, 8, 5 and even 3 dollars per share. A certain percentage of even these prices were based upon hope of the future.

If income can be materially expanded from the current low level, some of their common stocks stand the chance to occupy the position of the common stocks of Corporation *FFF* by 1935. (This is an example; not a forecast.)

IV. If it is good business practice for an individual to get out of debt (ultimately) it must be equally good business for a corporation to at least work toward that goal. The common stockholders never really own the business until the senior securities have been amortized. They own only the hazards of it. Between them and the earnings there is always that yawning gap, which in periods of low profits sometimes becomes very difficult to fill with its requisitioned share.

V. If a corporation's capital structure is heavily loaded with senior securities, the position of the common stock holders of that enterprise is more secure if earnings tend toward relative stability than

[91]

if they tend to vary widely from one year to another. (A railroad or operating public utility might not be "heavily loaded with senior securities" if 50 per cent of its capitalization—par value—was represented by such issues; the average industrial concern would almost certainly be over-loaded with any such distribution.)

Thus in all of the foregoing, the main point we have sought to emphasize is the increase in the hazard which the common stock holder carries when there are other hungry hands (bearing due license) reaching out to grasp substantial portions of net profit before his share becomes available to him.

This may be an unfavorable hazard or a comparatively favorable one. But note that it can only be *comparatively* favorable (*i.e.*, when comparing a good year with a bad one). Over a period of years, it will be found that a heavy weighting of prior obligations in a corporation's capital structure is more likely to prove an unfavorable than a favorable hazard for the common stock holders.

No attempt has been made to suggest when a corporation should or should not finance with senior securities; the going rates for money, the character of the enterprise, and more especially the condition of the security market and the receptiveness of security purchasers to various types of issues at various times, often become the deciding factors, despite the corporation's wishes or intensions.

Nor has any attempt been made to suggest how rapidly the outstanding senior obligations should be reduced; it has merely been pointed out that the best managed corporations customarily do make *some* headway in this direction—deny owners of the enterprise securities a certain portion of their dues today, so they may really own the business tomorrow.

A forecast of a long term decrease in funded debt and preferred stock is obviously, if that reduction be on favorable terms, a forecast of an increase in the long term value of the common stock.

4. NET INCOME

Net income available for the common stock is the financial item of cardinal concern to the common stock holder. Before he takes a long term position in an enterprise security he should be able to forecast an increase in this residue of gross and, if the principles earlier laid down are to be accepted as reasonable, this forecast should look forward to an increase of sizable proportions. The maintenance of the investor's position will—or should —to no small degree be conditional upon the realization of this forecast, and the ability to push it farther ahead in the future, with equally favorable implications.

Judged on the basis of its importance, therefore, net income available for the common should command more of our attention here than any other item. But in view of the foregoing discussions of the steps leading up to net, it need detain us now but for another moment.

It must have become obvious that the forecast of net must be conditioned upon a series of other forecasts. Among the most essential of these prior prognostications are forecasts of gross, of costs, of reserve policies, and of the size of senior securities.

In many cases it is not possible to determine all of these values or to express them in mathematical terms. But the forecasts themselves become none the less obligatory in careful security market operation. A projection of net simply *cannot* be even approached as a thing absolute in its own right. Net is a residue. To understand it, one must understand the other elements from which it comes. To forecast its trend, one must forecast the trends of its determinants.

To purchase or hold securities not based upon such forecasts, is not to invest but to speculate—and not even to speculate intelligently, but rashly, stupidly, blindly.

5. ASSET VALUE

The lamp post at the corner of Fifth Avenue and Forty-second street is a thing of value.

It has no direct earning value, of course; it is the lighting system as a whole, with its thousands of other lamp posts on other corners, with its great plants for generating electrical energy, with its underground system of wires for conducting this energy to its outlets, and with its exclusive franchise to supply light in certain sections of the city, that possesses earning power.

But even so, the single lamp post has its intrinsic value. It does the job that is assigned to it, *i.e.*, it reaches up twenty feet into the air and provides a proper outlet for the electrical energy generated back at the power plant.

It could be moved to some corner other than Fifth Avenue and Forty-second Street and do the same job as well. It could even be moved to New Haven, or Boston, or Montreal—provided its design was not hostile to that approved for lamp posts generally by those cities—and function equally as well as it now functions in New York.

Still further, having served the full term of its usefulness in its appointed capacity in any of these localities, it has still another value: its junk-pile worth. A carload of such lamp posts would fetch around half a cent a pound, laid down at Pittsburgh. The iron contained therein might readily reappear, in its next incarnation, as a steel beam in a new skyscraper or as a giant projectile whistling over the battle fields of Europe in the next war.

Worth in this sense is customarily referred to as "asset value." Sometimes the term "commodity value" expresses a similar idea even more forcefully.

Except where their liabilities exceed their realizable assets, all business concerns have a certain asset value to their owners.

Land upon which nothing has ever been grown or built has value of this kind. So also has a metal or mineral deposit which has never been worked, or the unexhausted portion of a mine already in operation; an industrial plant which has never turned a wheel or never earned a nickel; the stock of a bankrupt merchandiser; the inventories, equipment, and plants of a going and prosperous concern.

It is impossible to estimate, with any mathematical precision, the degree to which asset value reflects itself in security values.

As a general proposition, however, it may be asserted that neither the junk heap nor the commodity market is a suitable base for the issuance of securities.

This is merely another way of saying that the security owner must inevitably base the preponderant portion of his expectation of profit upon earning power. If he comes to the point where he must salvage what he can from the physical assets of his corporation, he is more often than not selling in a buyer's market, and under the most unfavorable circumstances possible.

As an example, the common stocks of not a few industrial corporations actually sold, as the 1929–1931 major bear market approached its trough, for less than the net quick assets of the issuing corporations. In other words, the market cared so little even for these liquid assets that it gave them a minus valuation. In one sense, this was like selling gold dollars for ninety cents. It merely emphasizes the importance which the markets usually place upon earning power. This is often an over-emphasis. Right or wrong, however, it does not alter the hard facts in the case.

Assuredly, the asset value of a business concern cannot be ignored in careful security analysis. When there is ground for suspicion that the current assets are a negative quantity, *i.e.*, are more than over-balanced by current liabilities, or even when there is ground for the belief that such an uncomfortable situation is being approached, an unfavorable signal of major import has been given.

But do not count upon a favorable asset position to give valiant support to a common stock in a weak market, or to be reflected in price to any marked extent at any time. Look at a favorable asset situation chiefly as a combination and arrangement of commodities capable of generating earning power, and then compute the probable degree of actual earning power that this combination can develop.

6. POTENTIAL VALUE

As has already been suggested in the preceding pages, it is peculiarly the function of the security markets to place upon value a time emphasis, and habitually this function is exercised by the projection of today's worth into the realm of tomorrow's probabilities. It is precisely for this reason that there arises the need for continuous reforecast. Hence we are accustomed to say that the markets are "barometrical," or that they "discount the future."

So far as the wish or the intent is concerned, these characterizations are quite correct; and this is as it should be. We have already seen that in numerous cases scant attention is paid to underlying asset value. Earning value is the dominant factor, especially in enterprise securities. But if the markets were not giving fully as much heed to tomorrow's earnings value as to today's, enterprise securities would, theoretically, be selling at zero when the corporations behind them happened to be temporarily operating at a deficit.

And so, in the stock market lingo, one frequently makes use of the term *earning power*. In this sense, power is synonymous with promise.

Security owners are willing to purchase such a promise, and often to stay by their commitments so long as the promise has any reasonable prospect of fulfillment.

Far from being a disruptive force, this urge of the markets to discount is something of a stabilizer. If investors revised their opinions as to long term investment values every time a new quarterly income account were made public, and if they changed their security portfolios to conform with such short term revision of opinions, the commission houses would prosper enormously—but the markets themselves would be incessantly pandemonium.

Moreover, the capitalization of potential value is not only strictly in accord with the long term viewpoint, but it is quite compatible with the most conservative methods of security market operation.

The careful security holder's eyes turn eternally toward the future. No system of evaluation can be of much account, no line of analysis can lead to any point of consequence, no long term investment program can promise any degree of satisfactory achievement, without full consciousness and acknowledgment of this underlying principle.

III
PRICE-MAKING FORCES

1. PRICE AS AN EXPRESSION OF VALUE

Preliminary to our preceding discussion of the gaps between gross and net income, the opinion was expressed that a significant relationship must exist between value and price, although not always so much as a 100 per cent relationship; and that the investor's problem is considerably more than half solved when the value enigma has been penetrated.

This statement is a conservative one. It fits into the preface to our discussion of price-making forces without calling for modification in any essential particular. It may be restated, however, in a somewhat different form:

Assume that price is the composite of a number of different factors. One of these is Factor V (value). Others are Factors A, B, C, D, E, and F.

Not always in the short term reckoning, and not necessarily in the majority of cases over the short term, but more often than not over a period of time, V will be greater than the sum of A, B, C, D, E, and F.

This is not only to say that over a period of time value is the most important single factor in price, but it is to go a step farther and express the opinion that, still referring to the longer term rather than the short term reckoning, value is more important in the determination of prices than all other factors combined.

It cannot be any other way. Were it not true, economic research would be an utterly valueless tool in the security market program. Were it not true, there could be no such thing as a scientific method of security market research, no such thing as a conservative investment program. Only the fools would buy common stocks under any circumstances; the wise men would direct their attention elsewhere.

Indeed, tested by every known principle of economics, we conceive this truth as such a self-evident one that an attempt to prove its validity could result in not much more than a multiplication of words. The bulk of the emphasis of this section, therefore, will be upon those factors which tend to *distort* price beyond the value relationship. In the discussion of these extraneous forces, further demonstration of the price-value thesis will from time to time appear.

2. THE MECHANICS OF A SECURITY PRICE

Of all the price information which comes to the business community, that relative to listed securities is the most accurate, the most complete, the most prompt, and the most widespread.

On the larger stock exchanges, every sale is a matter of official record. To those who are within reach of the network of ticker systems running from these exchanges, intelligence as to the price at which each sale is made is flashed almost instantaneously—under normal market conditions. So great is the country-wide demand for this type of price information, day by day, in more summary form, that hardly a newspaper in any important city dares to go on the streets without several columns of its costly space devoted to reports of the day's stock and bond prices.

From the standpoint of the owner of enterprise securities, the value of this prompt, accurate, and widely disseminated price information is twofold: first, it serves as a protection to him when he buys or sells, in that, within a relatively narrow margin, there can be no doubt as to the price at which the security owner's agent executed the commission that was assigned to him; second, it provides the security owner with a prompt and continuous check upon the price aspects of the value he may be holding, or is preparing to buy. Both of these are matters of considerable significance.

Meticulous or disappointed persons can, without much stretch of the imagination, find many complaints to bring against the technical methods under which various security markets are operated. It is fortunate that, except when conditions of the most extraordinary sort are dominant in the markets, none of these complaints can with justness be lodged against either the adequacy, the accuracy, or the promptness of price information.

In our later discussion of the various aspects of security prices, their relation and non-relation to value, and the hazards which prices themselves impose, it will be virtually impossible to produce a piece of clear exposition unless we pause for a brief prefatory description of the mechanics of pricing. Before we even begin to talk about prices, we must arrive at some understanding as to just what kind of prices are being referred to, and must have a common conception of the technique by which these prices are determined.

We shall be concerned chiefly with officially recorded prices of listed securities on organized stock exchanges, but shall not be unmindful of two other important classes of prices, viz.:

Unofficial and unrecorded prices of listed securities; and

Prices of unlisted securities.

A. OFFICIAL PRICES OF LISTED SECURITIES

No term could be more self-explanatory than "stock exchange." It is the function of such an institution to provide a market place, a place where the representatives of buyers and sellers may meet, and pass the wares of one client along to another, at a price.

Each exchange devises certain regulations relative to the types of securities for which it will provide a market, and indeed, names these securities, specifically and individually. It deals in these and in no others. These are called listed securities*; their names appear upon the list of the securities in which a given exchange declares it will deal.

The prices at which these listed securities change hands are those which are officially recorded on the ticker; on the so-called stock exchange quotations sheets which become available the following

* The term "listed," as here used, is not exactly correct, but its usage will serve our present purpose. As a matter of fact, some "outside" exchanges, such as the New York Curb, trade in certain groups of securities which they do not actually list. But these extraneous groups are definitely fixed, and are a matter of public record; hence we are justified, in the interest of simplicity, in referring to all securities that are traded in on organized exchanges as listed securities.

day; and which are summarized (usually by naming of the day's highest, lowest, and closing prices) in the daily newspapers and financial periodicals.

It has been found a matter both of convenience and of efficiency for various floor members of the exchanges to specialize in the buying and selling of certain specific securities. Thus every stock has a "specialist"—a member of the exchange who makes it his business to see that bid prices and offering prices for specific securities are systematically recorded. When the price which *A* bids for, let us say, 100 shares of General Motors Corporation common stock coincides with the price at which *B* offers to sell that stock, an official sale takes place, and an official price, for that particular transaction, has been made.

Purchases or sales "at the market," *i.e.*, made without the buyer or seller designating a fixed price, constitute, for all practical purposes, merely a technical modification of the process by which coincidence in bid and offering prices occurs.

B. Unofficial Prices of Listed Securities

An exchange is a matter of convenience to the investing public. Its members collect their fees because they perform a service that is desired— the service of facilitating exchanges of securities.

But security owners are not obliged to avail themselves of these services if they do not so desire. *A* and *B* can meet on the street corner, agreed upon a sale price for *B's* 100 shares of General Motors common, and then and there carry out the transaction. Upon notification and receipt of proper instructions, the General Motors Corporation's transfer agent will adjust its records to show official change in ownership.

Private transactions of this sort are most frequently resorted to in the transfer of large blocks of stock—10,000 shares of Stock *X*, 20,000, sometimes 50,000 or more. The prices are not a matter of public record. But these unrecorded prices often have an important bearing upon the future trend of official prices.

C. Prices of Unlisted Securities

The majority of corporations in the United States with securities outstanding do not have those shares listed on organized exchanges; but the majority of outstanding securities are listed—43,500,000 shares of General Motors common, 8,561,000 shares of United States Steel common, nearly 13,000,000 shares of Pennsylvania Railroad common, 11,640,000 shares of Consolidated Gas of New York common, etc. In other words, the largest corporations in the country with securities in the hands of the public have these securities listed, with the result that the aggregate market value of

[111]

listed stocks is considerably greater than the aggregate market value of unlisted issues; but the number of corporations which have sold unlisted securities to the public exceeds the number which have sold listed ones.

The dealers and distributors of unlisted securities are many. Sometimes they maintain a market for the issues they have distributed, *i.e.*, like the stock exchange specialist, keep an organized record of bid and asked prices, and strive to bring buyer and seller together. Sometimes they do not.

Sometimes a dealer in unlisted securities will become a specialist in a certain group of issues, which may have been retailed in the first instance either by himself or by some other dealer. He will thus be able to make a reasonably good market, especially if he himself participates in it, as a buyer or seller, from time to time.

Sometimes, on the other hand, an unlisted issue becomes an alley cat. No one claims it; it has no friends; no one makes a market for it; the owner, to all intents and purposes, is obliged either to find his own buyer, like the farmer with a horse to sell, or to part with his possession at a serious concession.

Prices at which unlisted securities change hands are not officially recorded. Prominent dealers supply to the press, and to statistical organizations, bid and asked quotations on issues in which they are interested. This does not constitute a guarantee actually to find a purchaser at the published bid price, nor actually to produce securities at the offering price.

The owner of an unlisted security is almost always at a disadvantage when he buys, and often so when he sells. He has no fixed standards against which to compare the price at which he buys or sells. He is likely to be obliged to make important concessions when he sells, and may, for all he knows, pay sizeable premiums when he buys.

During recent years the market for unlisted securities has greatly improved. The dealers have effected various kinds of organizations among themselves, and especially with the more important unlisted issues—shares of banks, insurance companies, investment trusts, etc.—have devised means for maintenance of markets which are quite satisfactory under normal circumstances. Naturally, in periods of panicky selling, and even in periods of hectic buying, these over-the-counter markets function at a great disadvatage. But it certainly cannot be said that the New York Stock Exchange itself added much to its reputation as the world's greatest security market during the Wall Street panics of October 24 and November 13, 1929, nor that during the insane buying which lead up to the September, 1929, peak in stock prices, did this great market provide anything important in the way of restraint.

Nevertheless, it remains indisputable that, on the average, the price hazard is materially reduced when the investor is making his purchases and sales in organized markets. Satisfactory markets are, as a matter of fact, maintained by unlisted dealers for only a relatively small percentage of the total of unlisted securities.

Further, most close students of price behavior will agree that regardless of its numerous shortcomings, the price hazard is still further reduced when one is dealing in securities that are traded in on the New York Stock Exchange. It is in times of stress when the maintenance of a market is most essential. Under such circumstances, the broadest market proves to be the least of the available evils.

3. THE BIDDING-UP PROGRAM

A sale of American Can common stock has just been effected on the floor of the New York Stock Exchange at 125.

Presumably, there is no more for sale, at the moment, at 125. But I want more stock. I bid 125¼ for another 100-share lot, and someone is willing to sell it to me at that price; I get my stock. I want still more. I bid 125½ for the next lot, and get none. I bid 125¾ and get 200 shares; 130 flat and get 300; and so on, over a period of days, as long and as high as I want to go. My success with my buying program will depend chiefly upon my resources: upon my financial ability to take, at the various price levels which I create, all of the stock that is offered to me.

Theoretically, I could carry this program on until I had purchased, in the open market, every share of American Can common that was for sale at any price. The final lot, constituting the last bundle of shares that anyone in the world was willing to sell at any price, might be taken in at a price of 500—even at 1,000. *My ability to pay for what I bought would be the sole limiting factor.*

This, in the simplest possible terms, is the essence of what is generally referred to, in Wall Street, as a "bidding-up" program. Please note particularly the qualification: "in the simplest possible terms." Specific bidding-up programs are so varied, both in their purpose and in their technique of execution, that they depart widely from this plain pattern. But our purpose here will be served by giving attention chiefly to the pattern.

We shall be content to distinguish only two types of bidding-up programs. The first we will designate as the *involuntary* bidding-up program. The purchaser is seeking to extend his interest in a given situation, perhaps even to acquire control of it or to become the dominant factor, and to achieve this end he finds it necessary to acquire a certain volume of stock. He is not thinking of immediate resale. His only purpose is to acquire the stock that he has in mind, at the lowest possible price. Naturally, he would prefer to extend his holdings either on a stable price level, or better still on a declining level. But in a strong general market this is usually impossible. Therefore he must meet a stairway of higher and higher offering prices. He bids up, but involuntarily so.

The second type we will designate as the *voluntary* bidding-up program. *The purpose is to acquire a certain volume of stock at one average price level, and to resell it, with as little delay as possible, at a higher price level.* This higher price level must therefore be created. It is voluntarily, purposefully, created. It is an integral part of the program.

Who undertakes a voluntary bidding-up program?

Anyone who has the necessary technical skill, the necessary knowledge of market facts, the necessary financial resources, and who forecasts that his own interests will somehow be advanced by such an operation.

Those remote from Wall Street have been taught by newspaper chatter to think of this nefarious business as being engaged in almost exclusively by those mysterious entities known as "the pools." A pool is a body of water often fed by a stream, and sometimes fed by several. A stock market pool is a loose and temporary association of individuals or institutions who pool certain of their resources (stock which they own, cash, credit, technical skill, etc.) and work together for the accomplishment of a common purpose, market-wise. It so happens that such pools have for many years past been regarded as among the most efficient media through which to undertake bidding-up programs.

The same results could be accomplished just as readily by a single individual, if his resources and technique were adequate, or by a single financial institution.

What is the sense in such a program?

It has one purpose and only one: the winning of a profit for those who engage in it. The operation can be a success only if the average resale price is in excess of the average purchase price.

This success depends primarily upon what is vulgarly known as "hooking the suckers" and more politely known as "attracting a public following." And this, in turn, is predicated upon the American security purchaser's incurable weakness for purchasing prices rather than values.

Sometimes a salesman puts on a red necktie. Naturally, this garment has no relation whatsoever to the quality of the goods which he is offering to his customer. But the fire-going cravat snares the customer's attention; that done, at least one hurdle has been passed. A common stock price movement itself, as day after day it continues to reflect an underlying bidding-up program, functions as a red necktie for those who are operating on the long side of the stock. It directs public attention toward this particular issue. Only a relatively few persons, of course, know precisely what is going on. Some of the others guess that the old army game is being played, and themselves take a position in the stock, hoping for the exquisite pleasure of what is called a "free ride," *i.e.*, to jump in quickly, ride along with the pool's program for a time (if it happens to be a pool that is conducting the operation) and get out again, with a tidy profit, before the pool has completely finished its job.

Often such price operations are accompanied by a series of favorable news announcements. When there are no such announcements, rumors have an uncanny way of permeating the Street. One hears whispers of vast hidden earnings, of new products of a revolutionary nature, of new technical developments which are going to effect great savings in costs, of prospective stock dividends or splits, of possible consolidations, etc. Thus there is ordinarily still another group of security purchasers which concludes it has discovered a neglected value; the price behavior is constantly confirming that conclusion.

But however it is done—whether by merely the red necktie of price excitement alone, whether by the opportune announcement of news or the opportune growth of rumors, whether by both, whether by disseminating the price consciousness which takes an upward movement during the recent past as tantamount to a guarantee of a corresponding movement over the near term future, whether by some other equally effective means—public interest *must* be aroused. This interest must be sufficiently strong to stimulate definitive action. The prospective customers must become actual customers.

In no such operation is it ever possible to effect any important volume of sales at the top price which is registered in the up-bidding campaign. No one ever hopes for such good luck as that. Stock is both bought and sold all of the way up. Some of it is gotten off at the peak (a sizeable lot of it, in the "right" kind of a market). Some more of it is gotten off after the peak of the movement has been passed. *The only requirement for success, so far as the up-bidders themselves are concerned, is that average selling price shall be higher than average buying price; the higher the better, of course.*

In the long bull market of 1921–1929 some of the most absurd situations imaginable developed as a result of operations of this kind. Often several groups were carrying out similar operations in the same stock at the same time. (Indeed, this is common in all bull markets.) Sometimes Group *A* would be half done with a program when Group *B* would step in and take the market away. Usually after a brief resting spell, one group was always ready to begin where an earlier active group left off. Think of the stark and absolute terror that must have slowly crept into the hearts of hundreds of gallant up-bidders in the autumn of 1929 as it became increasingly evident, week after week, that the public following to take off their hands the stock which had been accumulated in the final stages of the bull market simply did not exist!

The following principles, derivative from the facts surveyed immediately above, are pertinent to the present discussion:

A. The bidding-up program is one of the most effective of the price-making factors in the stock market. It is said that stocks do not go up, but that they must be *put* up. This statement is of course not entirely correct, but it has in it a sufficient amount of inescapable truth to engage our attention. At the very least it must be conceded that stock prices *do* move forward more readily when they receive a bit of the right kind of help.

B. This program often becomes a dangerous thing, but it is not necessarily an evil thing in the economic viewpoint or in the social viewpoint. Intrinsic value is one thing; public acceptance and public recognition of that value is quite another thing. The common stock holder necessarily depends upon price appreciation, over a period of time, to partially compensate him for the business risk which he assumes. That is an essential part of his program. Aid from any source is welcome. The fact that professional market operators win short term profits from a bidding-up program—when all goes well—does not contaminate the similar profits which automatically accrue to the by-stander who is holding the same issue, possibly purchased on the basis of a careful long term value analysis.

C. The chief danger lies in the fact that a bidding-up program almost inevitably distorts the price-value relationship over the shorter term. From the foregoing analysis it must be obvious that, granted the will, the promise of gain and a sufficient supply of capital assets, a bidding-up program can be carried to completion without much reference to value. But there is one saving grace in the situation. Not always, but more often than not, those stocks selected for market favorites are the ones which possess intrinsic value. For the up-bidder, the problem is half solved when he has selected such an issue. It is easier to attract the necessary public following with truth than with lies.

Therefore, those issues which really deserve to increase in price are, on the average, not interminably neglected by the pools. Those which do not deserve to rise in price receive more and more undeserved attention as a major bull market reaches the stage of climactic frenzy, but over a period of time they tend to settle at a price level which is more or less in accordance with the value facts.

D. A series of bidding-up programs, following one another in a major bull market, almost always carries prices to a level much higher than is ever justified by the value facts. It is the task of the successful investor to be not too tardy in recognizing this distorted situation. (Attention will revert to this principle in a later section.)

E. Thus in the longer term reckoning the bidding-up program becomes in one sense a price-value fact. Over the shorter term it is almost wholly a price fact. Careful investors must distinguish between the two types of movements; above all, they must not be lulled into that mute acceptance of things as they are which assumes all price facts to have the true status of value facts.

4. MAKING A MARKET

Something rather different from the bidding-up program may be inferred from the term "making a market," although the two fields of activity are quite closely related. The purpose in both cases is identical: financial gain.

Let us, as in the section immediately preceding, take a pattern case. We will say Banking House M has acquired a substantial interest in the common stock of Corporation S: say 20,000 shares out of a total supply of 200,000, or 10 per cent. This stock may have been purchased in the open market; it may have been taken over from a contemporary who was in distress; it may have been purchased direct from the company at an attractive price at the time some financing was done; it may have been acquired in any of a dozen ways; this makes no difference.

Banking House M has confidence in Common Stock S; has confidence in its intrinsic value, and is willing to hold it for the long term—say until this intrinsic value has become a matter of public recognition. Ultimately, of course, it may want to get out. But for the time being, resale is not a definite part of the program. The house is willing to hold until some distant date, when it can get a materially higher price than the present one; perhaps, if value continues to increase as expected, it may be willing to hold almost interminably.

Now, it must be obvious that Stock S will add nothing whatsoever to its general reputation as a "good proposition" if, during a generally strong market, its price has violent sinking spells. Nor will it add to its reputation if it does nothing price-wise in a strong market, nor if it is dormant on the sales activity side, nor if in a generally weak market it is allowed to sink more rapidly than the average.

In other words, in the protection of its own interests, it behooves Banking House M to keep an eye on the market behavior of Common Stock S. It does this by placing supporting bids in the market when weakness appears, and by actually taking stock—which often is later resold—at these bid prices. Conversely, in a rising market, Banking House M will not be slow to see that an appropriate amount of bidding-up actually takes place.

Thus when one makes a market for a stock, one *protects* the market for that stock. One looks out for it alike in periods of stress and in periods of boom, seeing that its price behavior does not become discreditable to the reputation that is to be built up.

This often results in an orderly market—the best kind of market that can be had.

"Market sponsorship" is another term which conveys virtually the same idea as making a market.

From this pattern, as outlined above, there are innumerable variations. We should say that the program of making a market is more likely to be a long term operation than is the bidding-up process as conducted by market pools; that the former type of activity constitutes a sounder and more tenable program than the latter; that the former expresses a real interest in underlying value more often than the latter.

Principles:

1. Market sponsorship is a price-making factor fully as important as the bidding-up process.

2. Other things being equal, a stock which has vigorous and effective market sponsorship over a period of time will give a more satisfactory account of itself, price-wise, than will a stock which is lacking such sponsorship.

3. The right kind of sponsorship, if it becomes a matter of public knowledge, itself tends to lend a lustrous halo to certain issues. Stocks that are generally known to be sponsored in the market by the bigger and stronger financial institutions attract a certain following for this reason alone. Hence:

4. In a generally rising market, the stocks known to have the strongest and most reputable sponsorship are likely to yield more easily to price stimulation than are those which bear no such reputation.

5. THE BIDDING-DOWN PROCESS

There is no operation in Wall Street to which the term "bidding-down process" is generally or popularly applied. The phrase is used here merely to set forth the idea implied as the antithesis of the bidding-up process, previously discussed in some detail.

One bids down for a stock when one bids for it below the going market.

In a major bull market such a program cannot, on the average, get very far or have much purpose. The force of gravity is all in the other direction. A below-market bid will not infrequently save the purchaser a few points as small, technical reactions occur in a forward market, and sometimes will save a considerable number of points in important intermediary reactions in such a market. But just as often, such cautious bidding results in the missing rather than the catching of purchase opportunities, and therefore costs more than it saves.

In a major *bear* movement, of course, the story is quite different. The common term applied in such a case is "accumulating on a scale down."

But note this: it is not the fact that a bid is placed below the market that makes the stock sell there. It is the fact that there are no higher bids. With the last sale of American Can common at 125, and with bids on the books for 5,000 shares at 124, 10,000 shares at 123, and 15,000 shares at 120, the next sale would in all probability be at 125¼ if there was one bid for 100 shares at this higher price.

In other words, no volume of below-market bids will force a price downward if there are a reasonable number of above-market bids. Just the contrary is true in the bidding-up program.

Thus the essence of the bidding-down program is not merely the placing of a bid below the going market, but *the short sale, which if it is successfully engineered creates a condition under which above market bids are impossible.*

Our present study is in no wise concerned with the technique of the "short sale." Every one knows what it is. You simply offer more stock for sale than the market will take at the going price. Therewith you create a lower price level. Then you offer more than the market will take at the new and lower level, then more and more. You hope that others who are watching the price performance you are engineering, as you press prices lower and lower by the volume of your offerings, will either follow your lead and join you in your program of short selling, or that holders of long stock will become frightened and offer their own supply

[129]

to the falling market. If they do, the party becomes all the merrier, the decline all the more rapid. Finally you get frightened yourself. You "cover."

There is no sense at all in offering more of your own stock than the market will take, in a short operation. That would be a betrayal of first-reader principles. So you borrow someone else's stock to "throw at the market." That is, you sell stock which you do not own, and borrow from someone else to make delivery to *bona fide* purchasers. You cover when you buy in the open market a sufficient quantity of stock to return what you have previously borrowed. Your bidding-down program, or short sale, is a successful operation when the average price at which you cover is lower than the average price at which you "went short."

Thus in two important respects the bidding-down program is potent as a price making force: (*a*) somewhat automatically, when in the absence of bids above the market a below market bid catches the next sale, or when a stairstep series of below-market bids catches a series of sales; and (*b*) consciously, when the agency of the short sale is employed.

Neither aspect of the program need have much relationship to value, in the short term reckoning. Both necessarily have relation to value over a period of time. The bidding-down process is merely one phase of the technique by which the market, over the long term, seeks to bring value and price into rough focus.

A falling market which is occasioned primarily because more long stock is being offered for sale than the market will absorb at the going price is something quite different. Where a declining price level occasioned by short selling might be considered an abnormality, or at least an artificiality, a similar situation when long stock was being offered to the market in greater volume than it would absorb should be considered a normality in every respect. In other words, a normal decline in prices has no reference to what we have here termed the bidding-down process.

All major declines in average stock prices, and perhaps the majority of intermediate declines, are normalities rather than abnormalities. Short selling is an important factor at times, and so also is the operation here referred to as the bidding-down process. But the preponderant factor in declining stock prices, over a period of time, is the simple, normal fact that sellers are more anxious to take decisive action than are buyers; concessions must be made to the buyers in such circumstances, just as they must be made to buyers in all other types of markets when the edge has been worn off their appetite for consumption.

6. PRICE AS A REPORT OF SUPPLY AND DEMAND

The classical economists define price as the point at which supply and demand equate.

It is an expressive and illuminating definition from the standpoint of theoretical economics and equally so in the view of security market economics. Obviously no other definition could be correct, theoretically. The fact that both supply and demand are often brought under artificial control in the security markets in no sense invalidates the application of this truism there. It is so in the wider economic field. Supply and demand have free play only in theory or under great stress. Commodities of all kinds, labor, capital, land— none of them moves to the market with absolute freedom at all times. With securities it is merely a matter of a greater degree of artificiality.

But it is when we seek to borrow from classical economics another term always used in discussions of supply and demand that we are likely to get into deep water. The reference is to the term "scarcity value."

In the broader economic field the scarcity of a good, *i.e.*, of a good which possesses real value, almost always creates an enhanced price. In the security markets, scarcity may be either a price stimulus or a price depressant—as likely one as the other. It depends upon the nature of the scarcity, and the method by which it has been created. Let us look first at the stimulating aspect of scarcity.

Patently, if the accepted definition of price is correct—and it should be accepted as correct—then, if the supply of a given stock at price level M equals zero, and if demand is greater than zero, the only conceivable way in which demand can be satisfied is by moving price up to M', or M'', or to whatever level is necessary to satisfy both buyer and seller. That is the only way in which a trade can be made. All security movements can readily be explained in these terms alone. But unhappily, the investor who has the desire to look beneath the surface will not be satisfied with any such easy way out. He will insist upon learning as much as he can about the nature of supply and demand at any given time.

During the great bull market of 1921–1929, high prices were in many cases explained on the basis of the scarcity value of stocks. We were told that certain stocks were becoming increasingly scarce:

1. Because investors liked them so well that they were locking them up in their strong boxes.

2. Because foreign investors were shipping them abroad.

3. Because big traders were setting aside portions of their purchases of the "best stuff" for long term holding.

4. Because the investment trusts were taking them off the market. Etc., etc.

All of which was quite true, and doubtless worked out as a price stimulus over the short term. But there were two things which were lost sight of:

a. Unlike wheat, corn, cattle, aluminum, copper, automobiles, pianos, lawn mowers, etc., securities are never used up. Actual supply offered to the market varies. But potential supply either remains constant, or trends to increase steadily over a period of time, as stock dividends are declared and splits are made, as new capital is brought in, etc. And:

b. The best laid schemes o' mice and men
   Gang aft a-gley
   And leave us naught but grief and pain
   For promised joy.

In other words, potential supply is likely to become actual supply at a moment's notice, and when it unexpectedly does so, all bets are off. Previously withheld supply may be forced to the market because of the owners' distress, or because of their apprehensions, or because the price level has reached a point that has satisfied their demands.

· Before following this line of reasoning through to its logical conclusion, let us turn for a moment to that type of situation in which scarcity becomes a price depressant, rather than a price stimulus.

There is at least one textile mill up in New England (doubtless there are several, but that in mind for the moment is singular) which not only managed to make some money year after year while the incomes of many of its competitors were sinking toward larger and larger deficits, but which in 1927, 1928, and 1929 was able to *increase* its earnings each year. This was indeed an extraordinary situation. The mill's common stock was traded in on the Curb. Due to the prevailing lack of interest in textile shares generally, it was never a market favorite.

An operator personally known to this writer "discovered" this neglected situation, this poor little orphan, in the spring of 1929. He promptly organized a pool to bid the stock up. This program met the minimum of resistance. It was greatly facilitated by the fact that the normal floating supply of the stock was relatively small. Fifty-one per cent of the total amount outstanding was

[135]

owned by the president of the mill and for some obscure reason was tied up in escrow for a period of years. This block could not possibly come to tbe market. Another 10 per cent was being purchased by employees on the installment plan, was held in the banks as collateral against loans, and was therefore also definitely out of the market.

This left a maximum possible floating supply of 39 per cent of the total amount of stock outstanding, and of course an actual floating supply of considerably less than that. Thus there was an implied scarcity value at the very outset of the bidding-up campaign. The situation appeared to be one which would be very easy to handle, market-wise.

At last the time came for our operator's pool to begin to distribute the stock it had accumulated during the course of its bidding-up program. It tried to do so at top prices—unsuccessfully. The public could not be interested. It tried to do so at a somewhat lower level unsuccessfully. It tried to do so at the average bidding-up price—unsuccessfully. To make the situation even more vexing, at and near the average price of the campaign, the pool was obliged to take more stock on the way down, to protect its own position.

Then, in September of 1929, the market as a whole became decidedly wabbly. In October came the first sickening crash. Distribution at a profitable price level became quite out of the question. The textile mill now had three groups of stockholders: the president, with his stock in escrow; the employees who were still buying on the installment plan; and our friend, who had been obliged to take over his pool's stock when the other members found themselves in trouble.

He still has it, and is quite unhappy about it.

The strange thing is that there is real value in the stock, and there was real value behind it in 1929. On the basis of average measurements, it was grossly undervalued when our friend's pool began to "give it a whirl," and the pool never pushed it up to a really unreasonable level, *i.e.,* not unreasonable for 1929.

The fact is that the supply of this particular stock was in such great scarcity under normal conditions that there was no general interest in it. As the pool took more and more, supply became scarcer and scarcer; trades became less and less frequent. There was no advertisement for it. Public interest dwindled to virtually zero.

There are many corresponding situations. Floating supply is often so small that it does not attract general public interest. Important groups cannot be interested in the proposition of making a market. Wise traders are afraid of the wide price gyrations that often occur between sales under such conditions. Intelligent long term investors, looking forward to the possibility that they may be obliged to get out on a declining market, with few friends of the stock to support that market, astutely stay away entirely.

Principles:

I. Over the short term, scarcity in one type of stock may prove a decided price stimulus.

II. Over the short term also, scarcity in another type of stock may actually prove a price depressant, by reason of the lack of public interest.

III. Over the longer term, scarcity is a wholly treacherous element upon which to pin one's hopes for market appreciation, because conditions both of supply and demand can—and do—change very suddenly.

7. THE PRICE-EARNINGS RATIO

One might wish it feasible to omit entirely this section dealing with the price-earnings ratio. Several of the conceptions involved are not simple. Their explanations required detailed mathematical calculations which, in this particular study, it is the purpose to avoid as far as possible.

But such wide use has been made of the price-earnings ratio, such inexpert use, such use as has lead to numerous basic errors in policy, that to ignore it would be quite out of the question. Therefore we may as well take off our coats and dive in, striving to make the discussion as non-technical as is possible, and trusting that we may come out, at the end, with a somewhat clearer conception of the uses of this tool than is now generally current.

The discussion will fall logically into the following main divisions:

A. The nature of the price-earnings ratio, and the limitations of its use.

B. Does it express a fact or a principle?

C. Reported earnings and disbursable earnings —the 10-times-earnings tradition.

D. The high ratio as a warning, and the low ratio as an invitation.

A. The Nature and Limitations of the Ratio

The price-earnings ratio is a very simple mathematical device. To derive it, one merely divides the price of a given share of stock by the annual earnings available for that share. With Stock Q selling at 100, and earning $10 per share per year, the price-earnings ratio is 10. Or expressed another way, Stock Q, at 100, is selling at 10 times earnings.

Thus the price-earnings ratio is a mathematical device used to express, in exact terms, the relationship between earnings and price.

Here we find ourselves in trouble at the very outset. Both in our preceding study of value and in our study thus far of price, we have seen that price at any given time assuredly reports something in addition to current earnings. It reports the hope of future earnings; it reports a certain amount of conviction derived from the past earnings record; it reports asset value to some extent; it reports various price-making factors which at times are quite remote from actual value.

So we must concede that a price-earnings ratio correctly computed from the mathematical standpoint inevitably contains an economic error, because the ratio reports only that portion of value which relates to current earnings. To that extent its value as a research tool is lessened. However, we shall here be dealing mostly with averages and with comparative situations, and it may be assumed that if our sample data are sufficiently comprehensive, the influence of this repeated error will tend to cancel out.

We are confronted with our second difficulty when we ask which earnings shall be used in computing the price-earnings ratio. Say that the problem is to compute the price-earnings ratio for Stock Q, which is selling at 100 on August 1, 1931. By what earnings shall we divide 100 to obtain our ratio? There are several reasonable choices:

1. We may use reported earnings for the last full calendar year, which in this case would be for the calendar year 1930.

2. Assuming that the company makes public a quarterly income report, we may use earnings for the last four quarters, which in this case would be for the year ending June 30, 1931.

3. We could take earnings for the last quarter, multiply by 4, and say that this figure represented the current rate of earnings, and use it as our divisor.

4. Or we could use what appeared to be a reasonable estimate of earnings for the full year 1931, based upon the facts that were available on August 1 of that year.

[141]

In most cases, the last suggested figure would seem to be the more useful one. A reasonable estimate of earnings next year (1932) would be still better, and a reasonable estimate of earnings for, say, the five year period 1932–1936 would be even better. But earnings projected thus far ahead could not possibly be "reasonable." So they must be counted out.

As a matter of fact, the time period selected for comparison is not a matter of outstanding moment, provided only that the computer take the pains to state what earnings he is utilizing in the solution of his problem, and provided his method is a consistent one.

In the examples to be used in this section, price-earnings ratios will consistently be computed from data which fall within the same calendar year. In other words, if we work from a price which occurs at any time in, say, the calendar year 1929, actual earnings (as later reported) for that year will be used. As this is written, earnings data for certain corporations for the full year 1930 have already been made public, while others are still only a matter of estimate. In relating 1930 prices to earnings, actual data will be used where they are available; estimated date otherwise.

On this basis, the accompanying long term record of price earnings ratios for a group of forty

CHART 1

COMPOSITE PRICE-EARNINGS RATIOS

(Forty active industrial stocks)

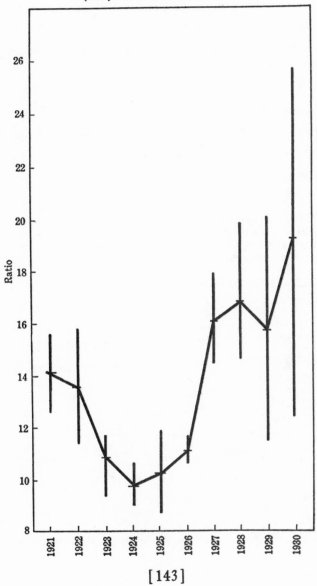

prominent industrial stocks has been computed. Two observations have been made each year: (1) based upon closing prices for the day upon which the Dow-Jones industrial average made its annual high, and (2) upon closing prices for the day upon which this same average made its annual low.

The composite figures report straight arithmetic averages of the ratios as computed for individual stocks. A test was made with weighted averages, but this method did not disclose any particular advantage as contrasted with the simpler one.

COMPOSITE PRICE-EARNINGS RATIO

(Forty active industrial stocks; two observations each year, on the dates on which the Dow-Jones industrial average registered its maximum annual highs and lows. Simple arithmetic average.)

Year	High	Low	Mean
1921	15.7	12.4	14.3
1922	15.8	11.4	13.6
1923	12.3	9.7	11.0
1924	10.5	9.0	9.8
1925	11.7	8.9	10.3
1926	11.4	10.6	11.0
1927	17.9	14.3	16.1
1928	19.8	14.4	17.1
1929	19.9	11.5	15.7
1930	25.6	12.8	19.2

The forty industrial stocks chosen for study were those included in the Standard Statistics Company's daily industrial stock price index relative to which it was possible to carry the record back to 1921. (This index is composed of a total of fifty stocks; it was necessary to eliminate ten because back records were incomplete.) Tests made with a larger number of stocks gave somewhat different figures, but revealed the same general *trend* over a period of time.

There will be occasion to refer to these composite data in several instances later on. For the moment, suffice it to point out that in computing price-earnings ratios one deals with two sets of variables, and that this fact, in conjunction with those previously cited, tends to delimit somewhat the usefulness of the ratio. The ratio changes when either prices or earnings change, or when both change; and in all cases, changes tend to vary over such a wide range that the ratio data themselves are seriously irregular, not only within a given year, but over a period of years.

B. Does the Price-earnings Ratio Express a Fact or a Principle?

When we report that Stock Q is selling at 100, that is merely a statement of a fact. It is merely a statement of another fact when we report that Stock Q is earning $10 per share, and still but a statement of a fact if we divide price by earnings, and report that Stock Q is selling at 10 times earnings.

But the statement of this latter fact might also, under certain conditions, be the statement of an economic principle, or at least the suggestion of a principle. For instance, if it had been established by research that stocks of Q's class and type should sell at 12 to 15 times earnings under certain conditions, then the mere statement that Q was selling at only 10 times would have suggested that an increase in price was warranted.

Is it, then, a secure economic principle, or if not a secure one, even a tentative principle, that under common conditions and at given times, price-earnings ratios for individual stocks tend to move toward an established average?

Or to frame the question another way: is there, at any given time, any reliable measuring rod for price-earnings ratios?

Let us look again at our average ratios, at two critical points: the 1929 peak, and the 1930 bottom. Certainly these situations were dissimilar in every respect. If we can observe any constancy of behavior either in the composite ratios at these two times, or in the ratios for individual companies, we will at least have grounds for the suspicion that there may be some underlying principle involved.

At the 1929 high, with the average price-earnings ratio for forty active stocks computed at 19.9, General Electric (the patrician of the group) was selling at 44.1 times that year's earnings, while

American Sugar Refining (the most humble of the forty) was selling at 9.8 times.

Now, the word average in itself means that there is something above it and something below it. That is what we always expect. But there is considerable question as to just what the answer would mean if one averaged the height of the Chrysler Building and of a two-story taxpayer; or the lengths of the Amazon and Hudson rivers, or the respective distances between New York and London and New York and Philadelphia. The extremes are so dissimilar that the means become more or less meaningless. Thus at a time when it takes $44.10 to buy $1 of the General Electric Company's earnings, and only $9.80 to buy $1 of American Sugar Refining Company's earnings, there must naturally arise some question as to the meaning expressed by a halfway station between these two points.

Take a greater number of samples. Take, at the 1929 high, the ten issues in our list of forty that were selling at the highest price-earnings ratios and the ten that were selling at the lowest ratios, and compare them with the average for the forty:

Stocks	Average price-earnings ratios
Ten highest in list of 40	30.2
Entire list of 40	19.9
Ten lowest in list of 40	12.3

These broader averages reduce the breadth of the dispersion, but by no means eliminate it.

At the bottom of the 1930 market, while the tendency was to cluster somewhat nearer the average, there were still such wide dispersions as to make the use of the average a very dubious measuring rod, viz.:

Highest P-E ratio in list of 40.................... 22.1
Average of 40..................................... 12.8
Lowest in list of 40.............................. 6.0
Average of 10 highest in list of 40................ 18.4
Average of 10 lowest.............................. 8.7

Let us leave these mere factual data suspended in thin air for a moment, while we turn to two other pieces of evidence that are to be introduced; then we can consider all of this evidence in a single block, and from it in its entirety can gather the threads that will be woven into our conclusions.

It has frequently been claimed that, over a period of years, the secular trend of average price-earnings ratios is upward, *i.e.*, that as time goes on, it takes more and more investor's dollars to purchase a dollar's worth of industrial earnings, and that this tendency will persist in the future.

Refer to the chart on page 143, which covers the period of the greatest bull market in history plus a year and a quarter of one of the most savage bear markets in history; note especially the light curve which connects the mean price-earnings ratio points for each year.

[148]

This curve dropped steadily from 1921 to 1924. Why? Because earnings rose more rapidly than stock prices.

It rose in 1925, 1926, 1927, and 1928 because prices advanced more rapidly than earnings—the exact reverse of the 1921–1924 situation.

It fell in 1929 because prices dropped more rapidly than earnings.

It rose in 1930 because earnings dropped more rapidly than prices.

In other words, here we have a trend line covering a period of just ten years, and *four different explanations* are necessary to account for its movement during that period. Often, in statistical studies, it is necessary to base tentative conclusions as to long term trends upon data covering a period no longer than ten years. Not infrequently the results turn out to be reasonably satisfactory. But it is not customary to base such conclusions upon data which require such a variety of explanations as the price-earnings data required for the period 1921–1930.

It is claimed that over a period of time individual stocks develop price-earnings habits, *i.e.*, that certain stocks tend always to sell at a relatively high price-earnings ratio, while certain others tend always to sell at a low ratio.

Referring again to the list of forty active stocks used in compiling our composite price-earnings ratios:

Six of the ten issues which were selling at the highest price-earnings ratios at the 1929 peak were also in the top ten group at the bottom of the 1930 market, viz.:

General Electric
National Biscuit
American Radiator and Standard Sanitary
Union Carbide
Allied Chemical
Sears, Roebuck

Five of the ten issues which were selling at the lowest price-earnings ratios at the 1930 peak were also in the bottom ten at the 1930 trough, viz.:

Bethlehem Steel
Stewart-Warner
Endicott-Johnson
American Sugar Refining
Paramount Publix

None of the issues which were in the top ten group at the 1929 high had moved into the bottom-ten group at the 1930 low; similarly, none of the issues which were in the bottom ten group at the 1929 high had swung into the top ten at the 1930 trough.

Preliminary conclusions:

1. The price-earnings ratio is a useful mathematical tool, but a highly dangerous one in the

hands of those who do not understand its limitations, and especially so when it is assumed to express a fixed economic or statistical principle.

2. It is not, however, without the *suggestion* of principle. (Further reference to this statement will be made in the two sections immediately following.)

3. Price-earnings ratios exhibit scant inclination to seek an average level. Wide departures from the average in either direction are sufficient to call for special study and are, as we shall later emphasize, even the basis for grave suspicion. But the use of an average price-earnings ratio as a measuring rod in any great number of situations is a very dangerous procedure.

4. A more fruitful field for analysis lies in the study of a given price-earnings ratio in relation to the factors attaching to that particular ratio than in a study of the relationship between a given ratio and an average.

5. The conclusion that the long term secular trend of average price-earnings ratios is upward is not without supporting evidence, but this evidence is in itself of such a nature that the conclusion must be very tentative, rather than final.

6. The principle—if such it is—needs to be tested in several more market cycles before it deserves general acceptance. In the meantime,

there is some basis for the assumption that price-earnings ratios themselves move in cycles, tending lower during the early stages of a period of general business and stock-market recovery, and tending to advance very rapidly during the later phases of such a period.

7. The contention that certain individual stocks develop price-earnings ratio habits is also not without its supporting evidence. But there is no guarantee whatsoever that these habits are inflexible, unbreakable, or eternal.

C. Reported Earnings and Disbursable Earnings

We must now turn attention to a phase of the earnings problem which has so far been completely ignored, but which is especially pertinent to our immediate problem. The reference is to the difference between reported earnings (*i.e.*, the earnings upon which ratios are commonly calculated) and disbursable earnings.

Following is a skeletonized financial statement reporting the composite situations of 493 leading American industrial concerns, as computed by the Standard Statistics Co.

Item 3 is the significant one, showing a balance of 2,371 millions after all payments to stock and bond owners, for the two-year period 1928–1929

493 LARGEST INDUSTRIALS

(In millions of dollars)

Item	1928	1929	2-year total
1. Net income available for the common stock.	2,543	2,951	5,494
2. Cash common dividends paid..............	1,414	1,719	3,133
3. Balance after dividends..................	1,129	1,242	2,371
4. Net surplus adjustments (*i.e.*, surplus credits subtracted from surplus debits)..........	403	328	731
5. Surplus for year........................	726	914	1,640
6. Net annual gain or loss in cash and equivalent, as revealed by composite balance sheet.................................	+761	−57	+704

On the face of the facts as stated, this sum was left over after all interest and dividend payments (common and preferred).

But the next item that meets our eye is an open admission that a sizable proportion of this sum really did not represent earnings at all. "Surplus credits" and "surplus debits" were made, with the debits exceeding the credits by 731 millions, thereby eliminating, at two simple little mathematical strokes, 32 per cent of the balance after dividends, as reported.

Fractionally less than 30 per cent of the balance after dividends (as reported) shows up in the gain in cash and equivalent. And this important item, of course, is the only portion of balance after dividends that is really disbursable to stock owners. The remainder of the indicated surplus went into inventories and receivables, or was "ploughed back" into property in other ways—all very good places for cash money to go, all having a possible bearing upon future earnings. But, it must be confessed, such employment of surplus earnings places the sums so used absolutely beyond the reach of common stock holders, at least for the time being.

Let us state the foregoing facts in a slightly different fashion:

During the two-year period 1928–1929, 493 largest industrial concerns reported 5,494 millions earned for common stock holders. This sum was doubtless earned for them, as stated, but it was not available to them, because only 3,837 millions (*i.e.*, cash dividends paid plus net increase in cash and equivalent) was disbursable. The disbursable sum was equal to 70 per cent of the total.

Here, then, there is revealed a situation of basic significance, and one of which many common-stock owners are not conscious.

Reported earnings are not necessarily disbursable earnings.

On the average, during the period 1928–1929, *only* 70 *per cent of reported earnings for common stock holders were disbursable.*

Therefore, an abnormally high market evaluation of earnings, as revealed by the price-earnings device, is even more dangerous and nonsensical than appears

[154]

on the surface, because the ratio as commonly com-
puted reflects reported earnings rather than disburs-
able earnings.

Example:

Corporation X is reporting earnings at the rate
of $10 per share, and its common stock is selling
at 200. By the conventional method of computation, the price earnings ratio is 20. But if Corporation X conforms to the average situation— *i.e.*, if
only 70 per cent of reported earnings is disbursable
—then the ratio of price to disbursable earnings is
not 20, but 28.6.

These data throw at least some light upon a
tradition which was highly respected in Wall
Street in earlier years, but which was cast rather
lightly aside in the glorious new era 1927–1929.

That tradition ran to the effect that a reasonably good industrial stock was "entitled" to sell
at somewhere around ten times earnings.

This premise itself must have rested, in turn,
upon another one—that, considering the speculative hazards involved, 6 per cent is a fair income
return on a reasonably good industrial stock.

Involved with both of these conceptions is the
further premise that, over a period of years, a
conservatively operated industrial concern can
afford to disburse in common cash dividends some-

where around 60 per cent of the sum that is reported, according to current accounting practice, as available for such dividends. We have seen that, in the two abnormally prosperous years 1928–1929, a maximum of 70 per cent of reported common-stock earnings could have been paid out to stockholders. The traditional 60 per cent figure, therefore, appears altogether reasonable.

Translated from percentages into dollar-and-cents figures, the foregoing means that, in the viewpoint of the tradition formerly current in Wall Street, an industrial stock earning $10 a share was entitled to sell at 100, and could safely pay out $6 per share in cash dividends, therewith yielding 6 per cent from the $100 price.

If, in a later era which has contemptuously discarded this old tradition, the price of a stock earning $10 per share has advanced to 20 times earnings, or to 200, it still cannot safely pay out more than 60 per cent of reported earnings in dividends (for reasons already pointed out) and therefore the yield drops from 6 to 3 per cent.

If the stock sells at 30 times, the yield drops to 2 per cent; if it sells at 40 times, the yield drops to 1½ per cent.

We shall develop this point more fully in the following section dealing with income return. For the moment, suffice it to point out:

1. That high price-earnings ratios and low yields are bedfellows—must be so, inevitably, due to the indissoluble relationship of earnings and dividends over a period of time; and

2. *That a price-earnings ratio which is not adjusted to a "reasonable" yield (whatever that may be—we shall inquire into reasonableness of yield in the next section) is symptomatic of a* POSSIBLE *grave distortion of the relationship between value and price.*

D. THE HIGH RATIO AS A WARNING AND THE LOW RATIO AS AN INVITATION

Are we, then, in view of the paragraph immediately preceding, justified in assuming that the development of a high price-earnings ratio should function as a warning, and that a low ratio should constitute an invitation to purchase?

In one way or another, an attempt will be made to answer this question in several ways, in several succeeding sections of this study. To avoid needless repetition and confusion of ideas, we must here put the cart before the horse, merely stating our conclusions and leaving the more detailed demonstration of their validity for later pages.

1. If Stock X is today purchased at a price which is 20 times earnings, it cannot conservatively

yield a cash income return much greater than 3 per cent, *and therefore net income available for the common stock must double before yield on today's price will become 6 per cent.*

2. Taking the periods as they come, over a long stretch of time, it is the exceptional American business concern, rather than the average one, which is able to double its net income every *five years*.

3. Therefore, if Stock *X* is bought today at 20 times earnings, to yield 3 per cent; if net available for the common actually does double during the next five years and if cash dividends have correspondingly doubled, the *average* income return over the next five years will amount to 4½ per cent.

4. When we begin projecting calculations on the basis of 30 or 40 times earnings, the yield figures become fantastic.

5. On the face of the facts then, a high price-earnings ratio IN TIMES OF PROSPERITY (say one greater than 20 times) constituted *per se* the grounds for grave suspicion. Certainly there will always be notable and numerous exceptions. But the investor who checks and rechecks his facts and his analyses whenever he buys a stock at more than 20 times in a prosperity period or whenever the issue he is holding rises above the 20 times mark, is assuredly not going to be wasting his time.

6. A low price-earnings ratio (say 10 times or lower in a period of prosperity and 7 times or lower in a period of depression) is not necessarily an invitation to buy, but it is, more often than not, an invitation to carefully investigate the *possibility* of making an intelligent purchase.

7. Used within such wide limits as these, and used by one who appreciates all its fallibilities, the price-earnings ratio is, as previously stated, a helpful tool in security market research.

8. PRICE AS A REPORT OF INCOME FROM DIVIDENDS

Consistently throughout this study it will be held that the safest price for a security is that one which reasonably reflects *current and prospective value*.

It will be recognized that common stocks are not purchased primarily for yield. Indeed, it will be recognized, and even urged, that the equity feature and the possibility of a long term increase in the value of this equity, is well worth paying something for—and therefore is quite entitled to be capitalized market-wise.

But at the same time it will be held that, over a period of years, the value of a going business concern to its owners bears a direct relationship to the sums that can be taken out of this business in the form of current cash income. It will therefore be held that income is never a factor which can be ignored.

In other words, precisely as in our study of the price-earnings ratio, it will be held that excessively low yields are fundamental warning signals— more often than not—and that reasonable yields are, at the very least, invitations to investigate the possibilities of a purchase.

The premise that a business concern's value to its owner must bear a direct and close relationship to the cash income that can be derived from this business rests upon the broader assumption that the earnings assets of capitalism can never be liquidated.

The "savings" of society are not reported by the sums that are on deposit in our savings and commercial banks. These deposits amount to somewhere around 50 billions. They are mainly "credit money"; the actual, or legal money in the country amounts to around $4\frac{1}{2}$ billions.

Contrast these relatively paltry amounts with an annual national income varying somewhere between 90 and 100 billions, and with an aggregate national wealth estimated at 360 billions.

This nation's real savings are reported in the accumulations, over a period of time, of that portion of its physical product which it does not consume—improved lands; houses and other buildings of all kinds; mineral deposits susceptible of being profitably worked; systems and devices for transporting human beings, commodities, electrical energy, gas, water; all types of mechanical equipment, etc., etc.

[161]

Now, it is quite obvious that an individual business man can liquidate that portion of the national capital over which he happens to have control. But he can do so only on two kinds of terms: (*a*) by finding a new owner who will allow a certain financial consideration for the privilege of taking over these assets, or (*b*) by merely "closing up shop" and allowing the chemical processes of rust and decay gradually to obliterate his assets from the face of the earth.

The latter course is seldom practical even for an individual, and neither course is ever practical or even possible for society as a whole, for reasons which are easily apparent. In the first place, society has no one to whom to sell its physical plant; in the second place, if its members are to continue to draw an income, the plant must be kept continuously in operation. Indeed, if this income is to increase over a period of time, the plant itself must continue to increase in size or productivity. (This is the dominant motive for saving.)

Similarly, security owners in the aggregate cannot liquidate their holdings. They may swap around among themselves indefinitely on changing price levels, but nothing more than that unless some method can be found for selling out *en masse* now and then to, say, the financiers of Mars. (As major bull markets approach the peak of their frenzy, the market captains rig up schemes almost as fantastic as this, but, thus far, not *quite* so fantastic.)

The acceptance of a low yield on a ccmmon stock means deferring cash income (from dividends) until some future period in the hope either that current sacrifice will be amply rewarded by the generosity of future dividends, or that the reward will come more promptly from price appreciation. The enthusiasm which, every five to ten years, carries stock prices to such unwarrantedly high levels overlooks the basic fact that security owners in the aggregate cannot sell out; the fact that capitalism can never liquidate its savings. If these elementary principles were called to mind a bit more frequently, there probably would be less current sacrifice of income; sensible investors would become progressively less satisfied with the 3, 2 and 1 per cent yields.

What Does the Market Yield?

As with the price-earnings ratio, yield is more of a fact than a universal principle. It suggests somewhat more of a principle than the ratio suggests, ordinarily, and pressed beyond certain trend lines either in an upward or downward direction, appears to be considerably more sensitive to certain economic laws. But such principles as are observable are always attended by glaring variations, and therefore must be utilized with the utmost care. Three per cent is not a dangerously low yield *per se;* 10 per cent is not an attractive generous yield *per se.* Both might be dangerous; both might be attractive.

So far as composite data are concerned, our examples in this section will be drawn from four computations:

1. The average yield on all dividend-paying common stocks traded in on the New York Stock Exchange on the days each year since the beginning of 1921 when the Dow-Jones industrial averages made their annual highs and their annual lows. This computation, involving some 9,500 individual observations, was made in connection with the current study.

2. Average yield on a varying number of "blue chip" issues (*i.e.,* high-priced market leaders), from the beginning of 1897 to date, as computed by Dr. R. S. Tucker and Colonel Malcolm C. Rorty, of the American Founders Corporation. The averages were taken at each year's high, low, and closing prices.

3. Monthly yield on 60 high-grade bonds, as computed by the Standard Statistics Company.

4. Various calculations relative to the yields on twenty-four market leaders during the five-year

period, January 1, 1926, to December 31, 1930, and projected over the five-year period, 1931–1935. These computations were also made especially for this study.

Data for the first named three series are set forth and charted herewith.

COMPOSITE YIELD, ALL DIVIDEND PAYING COMMON STOCKS TRADED IN ON NEW YORK STOCK EXCHANGE

(Observations based on average high and low prices each year)

Date	Number of stocks	Yield at year's high prices (per cent)
Dec. 15, 1921..........	113	7.32
Oct. 14, 1922..........	122	5.24
Mar. 20, 1923.........	164	5.86
Sept. 24, 1924........	182	6.44
Nov. 6, 1925..........	257	5.07
Aug. 14, 1926..........	209	5.76
Oct. 3, 1927...........	300	4.65
Nov. 28, 1928........	353	3.73
Sept. 3, 1929..........	388	3.53
Apr. 10, 1930..........	398	4.87

		Yield at year's low prices (per cent)
Aug. 24, 1921..........	99	9.17
Jan. 10, 1922..........	97	7.44
Oct. 27, 1923..........	139	7.51
May 20, 1924..........	174	7.36
Mar. 30, 1925.........	218	6.16
Mar. 6, 1926..........	239	5.62
Jan. 25, 1927..........	261	5.82
Feb. 20, 1928..........	321	4.56
Nov. 13, 1929........	408	6.69
Dec. 16, 1930..........	400	7.89

COMPOSITE YIELD ON SELECTED BLUE CHIP STOCKS

(Observations based on average high, low and closing prices each year)

Year	Number of stocks	Yield at each year's		
		High price	Low price	Closing price
1897	20	3.95%	4.98%	4.23%
1898	21	4.16	5.21	4.21
1899	22	3.69	4.39	3.92
1900	22	3.69	4.61	3.78
1901	24	3.40	4.33	3.44
1902	22	3.27	3.89	3.51
1903	23	3.64	5.22	4.58
1904	22	3.78	4.97	4.00
1905	25	3.29	4.03	3.44
1906	24	3.37	3.96	3.69
1907	25	3.87	6.45	5.78
1908	25	4.01	6.02	4.09
1909	23	3.44	4.31	3.70
1910	29	3.96	5.27	4.77
1911	28	4.39	5.28	4.77
1912	28	4.33	5.22	4.72
1913	31	5.42	5.81	5.42
1914	31	4.51	5.15	5.12
1915	36	3.78	5.21	4.07
1916	37	4.15	5.03	4.78
1917	42	4.60	7.34	6.62
1918	41	5.31	6.72	5.79
1919	44	4.33	5.96	4.77
1920	51	4.74	7.15	6.55
1921	49	6.27	7.43	6.29
1922	50	4.89	6.53	5.05
1923	46	4.88	6.27	5.66
1924	52	4.87	6.63	5.06
1925	58	4.09	5.60	4.40
1926	59	4.01	5.33	4.57
1927	63	3.78	5.15	4.05
1928	69	2.99	4.35	3.26
1929	75	2.00	4.33	3.44
1930	78	2.94	5.57	5.04

PRICE AS A REPORT OF INCOME FROM DIVIDENDS

Monthly Yield on Sixty High Grade Bonds

Year	January	February	March	April	May	June	July	August	September	October	November	December
1930	4.64	4.65	4.56	4.55	4.54	4.52	4.49	4.43	4.41	4.41	4.46	4.55
1929	4.60	4.65	4.69	4.69	4.69	4.73	4.73	4.74	4.76	4.73	4.70	4.64
1928	4.38	4.38	4.37	4.38	4.42	4.50	4.54	4.59	4.57	4.57	4.55	4.59
1927	4.54	4.53	4.51	4.47	4.46	4.51	4.51	4.48	4.45	4.43	4.42	4.40
1926	4.66	4.63	4.63	4.61	4.58	4.58	4.60	4.59	4.60	4.60	4.56	4.55
1925	4.78	4.76	4.76	4.72	4.67	4.66	4.69	4.72	4.72	4.73	4.74	4.70
1924	4.95	4.95	4.96	4.95	4.90	4.84	4.80	4.80	4.78	4.77	4.76	4.78
1923	4.86	4.89	4.97	5.00	4.98	4.98	5.01	4.99	5.02	5.02	5.01	5.01
1922	5.17	5.13	5.07	4.97	4.94	4.93	4.87	4.81	4.77	4.82	4.90	4.87
1921	5.80	5.88	5.91	5.90	5.91	6.00	5.97	5.85	5.76	5.69	5.50	5.29
1920	5.50	5.64	5.65	5.81	6.00	6.10	6.11	6.06	5.95	5.81	5.86	6.03
1919	5.14	5.14	5.18	5.20	5.17	5.17	5.20	5.30	5.32	5.28	5.39	5.48
1918	5.19	5.16	5.20	5.28	5.25	5.27	5.28	5.31	5.35	5.30	5.08	5.08
1917	4.45	4.51	4.54	4.63	4.72	4.77	4.81	4.85	4.96	5.01	5.10	5.19
1916	4.53	4.52	4.53	4.54	4.55	4.55	4.56	4.56	4.54	4.54	4.50	4.49
1915	4.68	4.67	4.68	4.65	4.67	4.70	4.71	4.71	4.71	4.66	4.57	4.55
1914	4.64	4.58	4.56	4.57	4.57	4.54	4.58	——Exchange closed——				
1913	4.51	4.52	4.55	4.60	4.64	4.69	4.72	4.70	4.68	4.69	4.70	4.72
1912	4.44	4.42	4.43	4.45	4.44	4.44	4.44	4.45	4.46	4.48	4.51	4.51
1911	4.43	4.43	4.43	4.43	4.40	4.41	4.41	4.43	4.45	4.45	4.45	4.44
1910	4.35	4.37	4.38	4.42	4.44	4.47	4.49	4.50	4.48	4.46	4.46	4.45
1909	4.34	4.32	4.34	4.32	4.32	4.32	4.32	4.32	4.33	4.34	4.35	4.36
1908	4.75	4.69	4.70	4.65	4.59	4.50	4.55	4.50	4.47	4.45	4.40	4.34
1907	4.26	4.30	4.34	4.36	4.38	4.45	4.47	4.55	4.59	4.68	4.87	4.83
1906	4.07	4.08	4.11	4.12	4.15	4.16	4.19	4.23	4.25	4.24	4.24	4.26
1905	4.08	4.06	4.06	4.07	4.07	4.07	4.06	4.06	4.05	4.06	4.07	4.06
1904	4.32	4.31	4.33	4.28	4.28	4.25	4.22	4.20	4.19	4.15	4.16	4.12
1903	4.12	4.11	4.14	4.17	4.17	4.21	4.26	4.32	4.33	4.32	4.35	4.33
1902	4.05	4.05	4.05	4.01	4.02	4.03	4.04	4.06	4.07	4.09	4.11	4.11
1901	4.10	4.09	4.06	4.05	4.06	4.04	4.06	4.08	4.07	4.08	4.07	4.08
1900	4.16	4.15	4.13	4.12	4.14	4.15	4.16	4.16	4.17	4.17	4.14	4.10

Observations relative to the dispersions of price-earnings ratios from the average, at any given stage of a market cycle, are equally valid so far as yields are concerned. With 388 dividend-paying

CHART 2

YIELD ON ALL COMMON STOCKS TRADED IN ON THE NEW YORK EXCHANGE,
1921 TO 1930

(At market's annual highs and lows)

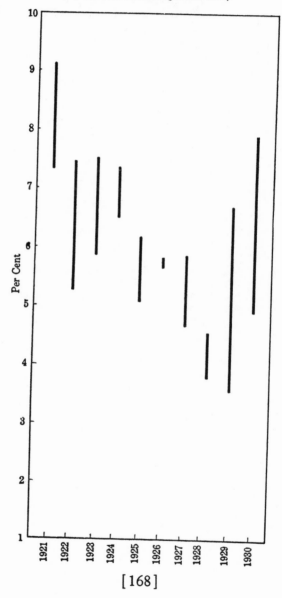

common stocks selling to yield about 3½ per cent at the maximum price peak attained in 1929, a substantial number were selling to yield less than half that amount, and numerous others were selling to yield twice the average or better. At the 1930 low, the dispersion was equally striking.

There is no evidence that the averages, at any given time, tend to function as a magnet toward which individual yields·are irresistibly drawn.

And the observation which was previously made relative to the development of habitual performances of the price-earnings ratios of certain stocks is equally valid—possibly even more so—with regard to the yield habits of certain issues.

In either a major bull market or a major bear market, composite yields on common stocks tend to conform much more nearly to a straight-line trend than do composite price-earnings ratios.

Refer again to the data reporting yields of all listed stocks at the highs and lows each year since 1921. Note on Chart 5, page 177, that a straight line, starting at the mean point on the 1921 range bar, and extended in such a direction that it passes through the lower terminal of the 1929 range bar (representing the point at which the 1921–1929 bull market reached its peak) gives a very good portrayal of the average trend for the entire period. The trend line on the price-earnings ratio ranges, on the other hand, plots out not as a straight line, but as a U-curve, with the right-hand ascender much more steep, and much higher, than the left-hand one.

The explanation of difference lies in the fact that yield is a more sluggish factor than earnings. Industrialists well understand that one bluebird does not make a spring. Despite the wide variations in earnings which occur from year to year, the tendency is to keep cash dividends on a much more even keel. In a bull swing, prices rise, relatively, much more rapidly than cash income from dividends.

The Flow of Capital

We may now turn attention to the data developed by Colonel Rorty and Dr. Tucker relative to the relationship between the yields on the blue chip stocks and on high grade bonds. Be it noted in advance that the difference in the yield on the blue chips and all listed stocks at any given time is mainly a matter of degree. The blue chips consistently range lower in yield than all stocks, but there is a striking similarity in the direction of movement (refer to Chart 4, page 174).

Accompanying the first announcement of this study was this brief analysis:

It is interesting to note that the average yield of these high grade stocks has fluctuated above and below the average yield of high grade bonds in almost every year, and that when the yield of the stocks remained below the yield of the bonds for more than a year at a time, there was always a severe reaction.

In September, 1929, the blue chips were yielding only 42 per cent as much as the bonds, but by the end of 1930 this situation had been wholly reversed, and the yield of the blue chips was almost as high in proportion to that of bonds as in 1907 and 1921.

Study of a ratio series based on the blue chip stock and the bond yields strongly suggests that when, in a cyclical downward movement of stock prices, yield on the blue chips closely approaches or crosses the 125 per cent line, a prompt reversal is due. In other words, when high grade bonds are yielding 4 per cent and high grade common stocks 5 per cent, historical evidence suggests that there will be an appreciable and effective volume of capital flowing, according to natural economic law, into the higher yield securities. (See Chart 3, page 172.)

Conversely, the ratio study would suggest that when common stocks are yielding only 75 to 80 per cent of what high grade bonds are yielding, capital, either perforce or by choice, shortly thereafter begins to flow out of the common stock market. This experience was repeated over and over in the period 1900–1927. In 1928–1929 when the blue chip yield dropped to 42 per cent of the bond yield, the reaction was delayed far beyond

CHART 3

COMPARATIVE YIELDS ON BLUE CHIP STOCKS AND HIGH GRADE BONDS

(The *A* line shows yields of market favorites, the *B* line yields of high grade bonds, and the *C* line the ratio of yields of market favorites to yields of high grade bonds)

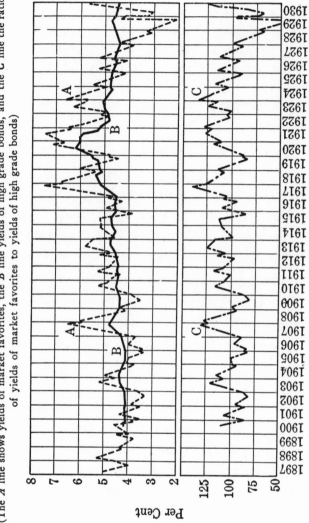

its customary term. But this is somewhat meaningless. The years 1928 and 1929 are now easily recognizable as sheer economic insanity, especially from the standpoint of statistical analysis. We have much to learn from these two years, but fully as much to forget.

Now, there is no disposition on the part of Colonel Rorty or Dr. Tucker to attach to the observations they have made relative to the relationship of stock and bond yields the security of infallible economic principles. Nor is there any disposition upon the part of this analyst either to accept them as such or to attach undue importance to his own further comments upon these observations.

The data do appeal to us, however, as of considerable significance—if for no other reason than that they fit in so well with mere common sense.

Certainly, there can be no dispute as to the fact that capital, over a period of time, tends to seek profitable employment. This is as basic as the two-plus-two-equals-four principle in elementary arithmetic. From this underlying conception, it is merely one short step to the assumption, less easily proved but in all probability fully as secure as the first, that capital would prefer more profit rather than less.

Accepting these two principles, then, the least that can be granted is that the demonstrated relationship

[173]

CHART 4

YIELD ON ALL STOCKS TRADED IN AND ON BLUE CHIP ISSUES COMPARED, 1921 TO 1930

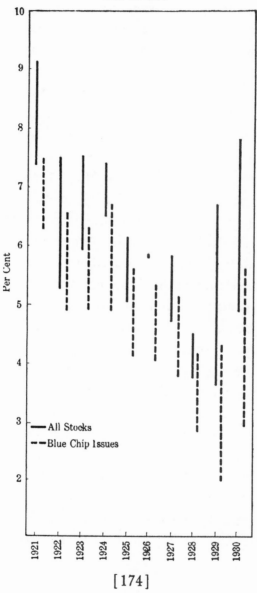

between stock yields and bond yields over a long period of years further strengthens the contentions (a) that there is a definite relationship between common stock values and common stock yields; (b) that when this relationship is seriously strained or distorted there develops a tendency toward a correction, and (c) that therefore the yield factor is to some degree influential in determining the trend of common stock prices over a period of time.

We say this is the least that can be claimed. We feel that more could be claimed without serious damage to any analyst's reputation!

It should not be understood that, in speaking of the flow of capital in the foregoing, there is any idea that money washes back and forth between the stock and bond markets like bromo seltzer that one pours back and forth from one glass to another in the process of making it fizz. The money which leaves the stock market at a given time does not necessarily step immediately thence into the bond market. Some of it, indeed, goes nowhere at all but into thin air. It is merely canceled as stock prices fall, or chalked up as paper profits as prices rise. The flow is not regular or immediate; it is irregular, halting, even meandering. The idea is merely that—presumably—under certain conditions there is a marginal and effective volume of money (effective so far as prices are concerned) that

[175]

prefers the higher yields and greater safety of the bond market, and a similarly effective volume which under other conditions prefers the higher yields, the longer chances, and the greater opportunities for profit offered by the common stock market.

YIELDS ON SPECIFIC STOCKS

The second statistical study toward which attention will be directed also deals with the so-called blue chip issues—*i.e.*, the market leaders which, both on the basis of the low yields upon which they sold as the 1921–1929 bull market reached its peak, and upon the basis of their market activity, were easily recognizable as the most favored and popular issues. The original study dealt with one hundred such issues. Later this was narrowed down to twenty-four, it being felt that this list was sufficiently representative to bring out the main points which it was aimed to emphasize. Of the twenty-four stocks selected for special study, all but two were selling to yield 3 per cent or less from their regular cash dividends at the 1929 peak in stock prices. More than half of them were selling to yield 2 per cent or less.

It must be recognized, therefore, that these were among the issues of which the stock market expected the most brilliant future performance. So

CHART 5

BULL MARKET TREND OF YIELD ON DIVIDEND-PAYING COMMON STOCKS

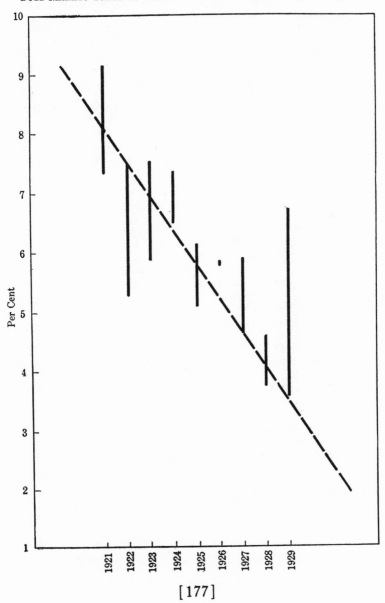

strong was this expectation, and so astonishing was to be the future performance, that their owners were willing to forego current return from cash dividends almost completely. Price appreciation was to supply the income that was lacking in dividends, as it had been supplying it for many, many months past. These are the stocks included in the study:

Common stock of:	Approximate yield at market's 1929 high, per cent
Air Reduction Co.	1.4
Allied Chemical and Dye	1.8
American Can Co.	1.7
American Power and Light	0.6
American Telephone and Telegraph Co.	3.0
American Water Works and Electric	0.5
The Borden Co.	3.3
Commonwealth Edison	2.1
Consolidated Gas (Baltimore)	2.2
Consolidated Gas (New York)	1.8
Du Pont de Nemours	1.9
Eastman Kodak Co.	3.9
General Electric Co.	1.6
International Business Machine	2.1
International Harvester Co.	1.9
Macy (R.H.) and Co.	1.3
National Biscuit Co.	3.0
Peoples Gas Light and Coke Co.	2.2
Procter and Gamble Co.	2.3
Public Service Corp. of New Jersey	2.0
Standard Gas and Electric	1.7
Standard Oil Co. of New Jersey	2.7
United Gas Improvement Co.	1.5
U. S. Gypsum Co.	1.8
Average yield	1.9

The thought was to go back over the five-year period, 1926–1930, and carefully determine just what these common stocks actually had produced for their owners, in the way of cash dividends; then to project whatever trend line might be established into the future—say over the five-year period, 1931–1935. It was felt that if past performance could be demonstrated to be as brilliant as the market itself apparently assumed at its 1929 high, that the 1, 2, and 3 per cent yields then prevailing might be at least partially justified.

Our contention will be that on the average a price which reports a 3 per cent yield on a common stock is likely to be a dangerous price; that a price which reports a 2 per cent yield is much more likely to be dangerous; that a price which reports a 1 per cent yield is silly, fantastic, and unjustifiable, and should not be countenanced by the conservative investor under even the most extraordinary circumstances. (When we drop down to the zero yields —*i.e.*, to the non-dividend payers—we are dealing with another kind of investment risk entirely, consideration of which need not complicate the immediate inquiry.)

But it will be observed that we are giving the other side of the argument, if such there be, "all of the breaks." Our examples are being drawn from a group of the highest grade stocks on the Board—a group which, both from the standpoint of price appreciation, increase in earnings, and increase in dividends, has for years past been far out in front of the broad averages.

It will be noted also that the period selected for study was one of the most prosperous five-year periods in this country's economic history. During the first four years of this half decade, the flood of prosperity rose steadily, reaching an absolutely unprecedented crescendo in 1929. The year 1930 was a sizable step down, but much more so from the standpoint of earnings than from that of dividends—and it is with dividends that we are here chiefly concerned.

Further, during this same period, new capital was available to prosperous corporations in almost unlimited quantities. Up until the autumn of 1929, no "rights" were offered which were not avidly exercised. And market conditions were especially favorable for the under-cover increase in cash dividends by the routes of stock splits, stock dividends, etc.

In other words, we are here examining the dividend histories of an especially prosperous group of corporations, especially favored by purchasers of common stocks, operating under especially favorable conditions, both from the industrial and the financial standpoint. The companies themselves are ahead of the average company; the period under examination was greatly more prosperous than the average five-year period in our economic history. Thus it would seem reasonable to assume that the results achieved by these corporations, under the prevailing conditions, would be about the *best* that could possibly be hoped for. The line of expectation for the *average company* would run somewhat lower. The line of expectation for these particular companies operating over an *average five-year period* would likewise run somewhat lower. The line of expectation for the *average company operating over an average period* would run appreciably lower.

We assume that, at the beginning of the five-year period under survey, *i.e.*, on January 1, 1926, the Wise Investor purchased one share each, at the market, of each of the twenty-four common stocks on our list.

His cash lay-out would have amounted to $3,078; his aggregate cash income from dividends would have been at the rate of $122 per year, and his yield at his purchase prices would have averaged 3.97 per cent.

We assume that the Wise Investor not only held his investments intact throughout the next five years, but that he accepted and retained all stock dividends that were made and, moreover, that when rights were offered to him, he came forth with sufficient funds to exercise all of them. The exercise of his rights cost him $456.75. His total cash lay-out over the five-year period, therefore, amounted to $3,535.

During the period, he received $1,054 in cash dividends.

At the end of the period he was receiving $167 more in cash dividends than at the beginning. This represented an increase of 137 per cent, equivalent to an annual average increase of about 27½ per cent.

Making due allowance for the additional sums that were advanced in the exercise of rights, and paying due heed to the time at which these payments were made, the Wise Investor's *annual average return on his total investment over the entire five-year period, 1926–1930—i.e., of course, his income return from cash dividends—amounted to 6.38 per cent.*

Considering the high calibre of the issues involved, the fancy prices which the market was willing to place on them, and the prosperity characteristics of the period under study, an average five-year income return amounting to 6⅓ per cent would appear shockingly low.

The other side of the question, of course, is that the Wise Investor would have been more than compensated for this forbearance of income from dividends by his capital gains. With the acceptance of his stock dividends and the exercise of his rights he would have held 84½ shares of stock on December 31, 1930, as compared with the twenty-four shares which he held at the outset. And even with the depreciated values which obtained on December 31, 1930, following the savage major bear market of 1929–1930, these 84½ shares could have been sold for 87 per cent more than they cost.

The question at issue is whether any system of market evaluation, which even in a period of unprecedented prosperity allows a 6 per cent dividend return from a group of twenty-four leading stocks is a sound system of evaluation—whether it is a system which can be counted upon to endure over a longer period of time.

Our assumption is that it is not. We believe that in an average five-year period, the common stock investor carries a sufficiently great hazard to entitle him to a higher cash dividend return.

The case becomes even more clear if we begin to shuffle our periods somewhat.

Assume that the rate of increase in dividend increases established by these twenty-four corporations during the period 1926–1930 is a permanent rate for any five-year period. This in itself is a rash assumption, because hardly any careful analyst believes that the rate of growth established during the abnormally prosperous 1926–1930 period can be maintained over a long term of years. But assume that it might be, merely for the sake of illustration.

Then assume that a Not So Wise Investor had come into the market on September 7, 1929—the day on which the 1921–1929 market reached its all-time peak. He purchases one share of stock of each of the twenty-four concerns on our list. His current yield was slightly under 2 per cent.

Project the situation five years ahead, basing the projection on the rate of increase established during the five-year period 1926–1930.

On this basis, and at his September 7, 1929 purchase price, the Not So Wise Investor could look forward to a dividend return yielding him 4.17 per cent 5 years hence, and to an annual average yield of 3.14% on his investment.

No one expects the next five years to equal the past five years in corporate dividend-paying ability. So let's be conservative and write this projected yield figure named immediately above down to 2½ per cent.

And at that point we reach absurdity. Quite regardless of whether 6⅓ per cent might be considered a satisfactory five-year return from dividends on leading blue chip stocks, we take it that no one will quarrel with the statement that a return of only slightly more than 3 per cent could *not* be considered satisfactory by any stretch of the imagination.

Granting again that common stocks are not purchased primarily for yield, it still remains true that *over a period of years* the values of these stocks must bear *some* relationship to the amount of cash dividends that can be derived from them; yield must under certain conditions be a price-making factor.

The reason yield has not in the past been more vital as a price-making factor is because so few investors have taken the trouble to calculate long-term future probabilities.

When you buy or hold a common stock that returns a yield of 3 per cent or less from its cash dividend, look ahead a few years and try to determine whether your present sacrifice has at least an even chance to be compensated for later on. If you cannot convince yourself that the situation does hold this probability, some vital readjustments in your position may prove to be in order.

When you buy or hold a common stock that yields you 6 to 7 per cent or better, when the prospect is that this yield will at least be maintained and that it will probably be increased over a period of time, your investment position will, on the average, prove to be infinitely more secure than if it were on the lower yield basis.

9. PRICE AS A REPORT OF THE AVAILABLE SUPPLY OF CREDIT

As has befallen so many other characters in economic literature, *A* and *B* are shipwrecked on a desert island.

A has two dollars and a half in his pocket. *B* has nothing. After a time, *A*'s overcoat wears out, and he opens negotiations to purchase *B*'s, for real money.

Obviously, the price at which the overcoat will pass from *B* to *A* will lie somewhere between one cent and two dollars and a half. It cannot conceivably exceed the last named figure because that is all of the money there is in *A*'s and *B*'s world. This is the "money problem" in its very simplest terms.

In the security markets the working of the principle is basically the same, although slightly more complicated by the introduction of the credit element. But if it is true that, with only two dollars and a half available in *A*'s and *B*'s island world the price of *B*'s overcoat cannot possible exceed that sum, it is likewise true that no matter how complex may be the financial organization of a civilized society, the prices of the goods and services which change hands must bear a close relationship to the volume of cash and credit money which this society possesses.

It happens that especially designated types of credit are available to security buyers. If the purchaser finances his operations at his commercial bank, he usually makes a "collateral loan." If he calls upon his broker to finance him, the broker borrows from a commercial bank, or, with the bank usually acting as an intermediary, from a corporation or individual. This too is a collateral loan, but is generally known as a "broker's loan." The great majority of brokers' loans are callable at the option of the lender, and are therefore spoken of as "call loans."

This latter type of credit is therefore more sensitive and more flexible than any other type. Call loans to brokers may rightly be said to constitute the dominant credit factor in the common stock markets.

The accompanying chart compares the trend of brokers' loans, from the beginning of 1926 to the end of 1930, with the aggregate market values of the 404 common stocks included in the Standard Statistics Company's weekly index. It will be observed that the *direction* of the two curves is identical for all practical purposes, although the

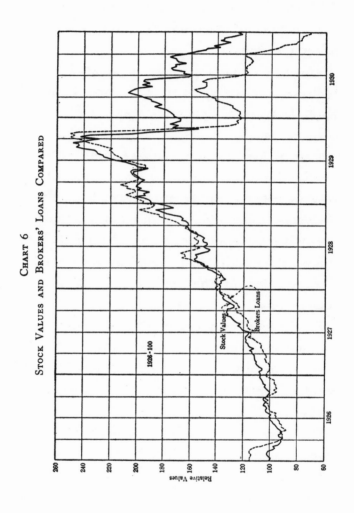

CHART 6

STOCK VALUES AND BROKERS' LOANS COMPARED

1926=100

Stock Values

Brokers Loans

Relative Values

spread between their respective positions is a variable.

To no small degree, the situation is a case of interaction. More and more credit must be extended as stock prices mount higher and higher. Otherwise, prices *could not rise*. Less and less credit is needed as prices decline.

Does the egg come from the chicken, or the chicken from the egg? Do the larger loans make the higher stock prices, or the higher stock prices make the larger loans? The exact answer would be rather meaningless. But what *must* be recognized is that the volume of security loans over a period of time is a price-making factor in the common stock market. Without an expansion in loans, stock prices could not rise—or, to be a trifle more exact, they could not experience a *major* advance without an expansion in loans.

Conversely, an important contraction in the volume of loans available to security buyers must inevitably result in a marking down of prices. There is now no doubt whatsoever that the two panics which occurred in the stock market successively in October and November, 1929, were to no small extent occasioned by the wholesale calling of stock market loans by banks, individuals, and corporations that had suddenly become dubious as to the safety of their commitments.

[189]

The rate of interest is only one of several factors influential in determining the volume of credit that shall be available to the security markets. Broadly speaking we may say that:

1. Any series of events or circumstances which occasions either a strain or a contraction in the volume of credit that is available to security buyers constitutes a bear point in security prices.

2. Any series of events or circumstances which provides security buyers with the opportunity to enlarge their borrowings constitutes a bull point in the price structure.

3. The effects of a tight situation are likely to exhibit themselves more promptly in the price structure than the effects of easy money. Or in other words, tight, unexpansive credit is in itself sufficient to break a bull movement in prices; easy credit is permissive of rising prices, but ordinarily must be supplemented by other favorable factors before the prices begin decisively to rise.

In the foregoing sections dealing with price-making forces we have referred to only a relatively small number of the more important ones. Necessarily, those which have been omitted are legion. If reference were made to all of the multitude of statistical calculations and series that have been painfully worked out in the endless search for the determinants of stock prices, the material would not occupy a portion of a single volume, but all of dozens of volumes. And the purpose to be served probably would be well summarized in the recent quip of a Wall Street wag:

"If all the statisticians in the United States were laid end to end they would reach from New York to Washington—and that would be a jolly good thing!"

In both the preceding sections dealing with value and with prices, an effort has been made to utilize only such data as are generally available to the average business man, if he will make the modicum of effort to possess himself of them. Esoteric data are patently not to the purpose of the average investor, nor of this study.

In the sections immediately following it is the plan to utilize such data as have already been presented, along with such additional data as are needed, in the outlining of a conservative long term common stock investment program. Attention is again called to the fact that the common-stock program is not assumed ever to constitute more than a *portion* of the *entire* investment program.

IV
CARRYING THE PRICE-VALUE RISK

1. DISTINCTIVE TYPES OF LONG TERM PRICE FLUCTUATION

If there could be such a thing as a static economic society, common stocks, theoretically, would have virtually the same status as bonds. Values would not change much from year to year, since within this static society the volume of demand for goods and services would not vary, nor would the volume of goods produced for sale vary, nor the level of commodity prices, nor interest rates, nor the margin of profit, etc.

In a retrogressive economy, common stocks would in theory be eternally declining, on the average, and therefore would constitute the poorest possible investment.

It is in a progressive economy that common stocks increase in value the most rapidly. Here in the United States we have enjoyed the spectacle of an economy which during the last century has probably progressed farther and more rapidly than any other on the earth.

Every investor who holds common stocks at the present time forecasts that this progress which has been a matter of historical fact during the past will continue into the long term future.

[195]

This hypothesis, indeed, must inevitably lie at the very base of every intelligently prosecuted long term common stock investment program. Whether it is a valid hypothesis no human being can know with absolute certainty. In the light of historical experience and in the absence of any conclusive evidence to the contrary, the burden of proof is upon those who question its validity, rather than upon those who accept it.

The hypothesis is accepted at its full face value for the purposes of this study, and all subsequent assumptions are based upon this primary one; there is simply nothing else to do but accept it, in the light of known facts.

Now, economic progress has certain definite characteristics. One of these characteristics is that an economy does not, over a period of years, progress steadily or evenly. The tempo of progress, in other words, is uneven: sometimes slow and measured; sometimes rapid and spectacular—indeed, at times so very rapid that corrective retrogression must occur before progress can resume.

That is to say, economic progress is a fluctuating force. On balance and over a period of time, the upward fluctuations are greater in degree than the downward ones. In a retrogressive economy it is precisely the reverse: on balance, the downward fluctuations are greater than the upward ones. In the theoretic static economy, the two would tend to equate.

In any conservative long term investment program it is necessary for the investor to recognize and identify certain distinctive types of fluctuation. If these could be illustrated on the basis of value—that is, if the examples which are to be here cited could be examples of different kinds of value fluctuation—our purpose would be served much the better. But this is impractical. So we are obliged to fall back upon certain types of price fluctuation, as they are manifest in the records of the stock market. However, if the reader will bear in mind that price reflects value to a considerable degree over a period of time, and that virtually the same results could be obtained if value facts were available from day to day or even from month to month, we will come out at approximately the same end.

A. The Major Cyclical Fluctuation

The study of the so-called business or stock market cycles has engaged its full share of the attention of resourceful economists and statisticians during the past few decades. Justly so; fortunately so. Perhaps there is no other single business phenomenon which it is so important to understand.

We may here summarize the conclusions of the students of cyclical phenomena with the utmost brevity—with a brevity which, we make so bold as to hope, establishes a world record:

The majority (i.e., more than 50 per cent) of business situations tend to fluctuate in the same direction at the same time—upward, downward, or horizontally.

The students of cyclical phenomena are concerned not with the so-called short term movements which occur in business, but with the longer ones, each usually extending over a period of years. Specifically, one cycle in business is measured either from one period of prosperity to the next period, or from one period of depression to the next. A complete cycle takes in both a period of prosperity and a period of depression.

In a general way, the prices of common stocks move in cycles corresponding, roughly, with the cycles in general business activity. A complete cycle in the stock market includes both a major bull market and a major bear market. Not all common stocks, but the majority (*i.e.*, more than 50 per cent) move in the same general direction at the same time.

Chart 7 accompanying depicts the course of average common stock prices from the beginning of the present century to mid-1931. The cycles,

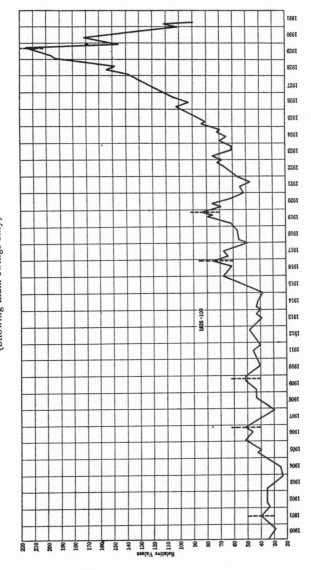

CHART 7

LONG TERM TREND OF COMMON STOCK PRICES
(Showing main swings only)

as measured from the peak of one major bull market to the peak of the next, are indicated by the broken horizontal lines. The curve shows only the more important swings in the market; the smaller, or minor movements are ignored.

B. Fluctuation within a Given Industry Which Conforms with the Average

If the tide of prosperity is rising in the majority of business situations, it is necessarily rising in the average situation, and likewise is necessarily rising in the average subdivision of business, or industry.

This means that the majority of individual corporations operating in a given industry, in a period of rising prosperity, are expanding their profits—or, in other words, that the profits of the industry as a whole are expanding.

Common stocks of the leading concerns operating within a single industry are sometimes referred to as a "stock group." Chart 8 accompanying depicts the courses (*a*) of the average price of 404 leading stocks of all kinds during the period January, 1928–September, 1929 (*i.e.*, the course of the stock market as a whole); (*b*) the course of the average price of ten leading stocks in the steel group, and (*c*) the course of the average price of nine stocks in the chemical group. These are typical examples

CHART 8

STEEL AND CHEMICAL GROUPS COMPARED WITH TREND OF 404 LEADING STOCKS

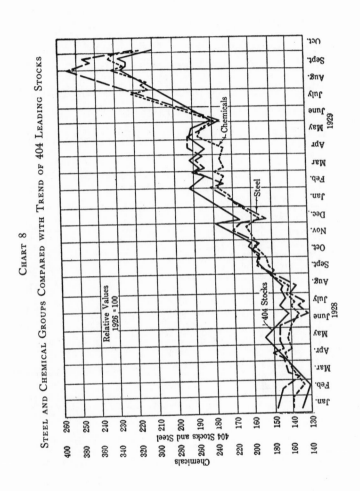

of groups of stocks which, in a general way, fluctuate with the stock market as a whole.

C. FLUCTUATION IN AN INDIVIDUAL SITUATION WHICH CONFORMS WITH THE BROAD AVERAGE AND THE GROUP AVERAGE

It has already been pointed out that the majority of individual common stocks tend to fluctuate with the stock market as a whole. Indeed, this is

CHART 9

U. S. STEEL CORPORATION'S COMMON STOCK COMPARED WITH TREND OF 404 LEADING STOCKS

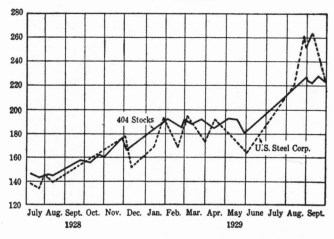

necessarily why the so-called stock market as a whole develops a trend in any given direction— simply because the majority of stocks develop a common trend.

A typical example of this type of fluctuation is observable in the case of the common stock of the

United States Steel Corporation, the market price
of which is compared with the average price of
404 stocks in Chart 9. The details, or shorter term
movements do not correspond; throughout the
period for which observations have been reported
the general direction of movement is the same.

D. GROUP FLUCTUATIONS WHICH DO NOT
CONFORM WITH THE BROAD AVERAGE

Chart 10 illustrates this type of fluctuation very
nicely. The stock market as a whole, as portrayed

CHART 10

AUTOMOBILE, LEATHER, RAYON AND TOBACCO GROUPS COMPARED WITH
TREND OF 404 LEADING STOCKS

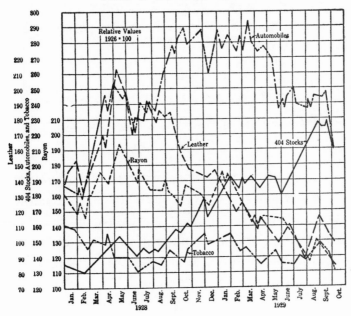

by the average price of 404 leading stocks, reached its peak in September, 1929, and, for all practical purposes, may be said to have risen continuously throughout the preceding 20 months.

Leather and rayon stocks, on the other hand, reached their peaks on a major bull movement in the first half of 1928, and declined continuously for more than a year, while the market as a whole was mounting higher and higher.

Automobile stocks reached their cyclical peak in late March, 1929, and declined drastically during the next four months, while the market as a whole went on rising.

Tobacco stocks followed a sidewise movement while the market as a whole was negotiating its 1928–1929 rise.

E. Fluctuation in an Individual Situation Which Conforms with a Nonconforming Group Fluctuation

In view of the foregoing, this type of fluctuation is too obvious to call for illustration. While the leather group was moving downward in the last half of 1928 and throughout 1929, the common stock of American Hide and Leather was moving in the same general direction.

F. Fluctuation in an Individual Situation Which Conforms Neither with Its Group nor with the Broad Average

In other words, fluctuation which conforms with nothing that it should conform with. This type of movement is beautifully illustrated by the price behavior of Chrysler Motor common stock, which,

CHART 11

CHRYSLER MOTOR COMMON COMPARED WITH TREND OF 404 LEADING STOCKS

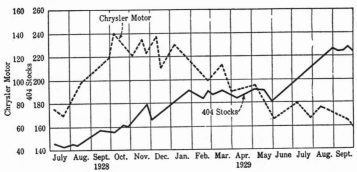

as they say in Wall Street, was "given a whirl" shortly after the Dodge consolidation. The performance seems to have been artificial in certain respects; some very harsh words were spoken about it at the time it occurred.

In mid-July, 1928 (pending final details of the Dodge consolidation, in which the holders of Dodge preferred stock were obliged to exchange their senior shares for Chrysler common) Chrysler common was available in the market at below 70.

Just twelve weeks later the price had been doubled —pushed up to 140. This marked the price peak for the bull market. Thereafter the main trend of Chrysler common was downward, although it was held near the peak for a number of weeks, giving those who had operated the pool an ample chance to distribute a heavy volume.

The average stock in the automobile group did not reach its cyclical peak until almost six months after Chrysler common had touched its high; the average stock on the stock exchange as a whole did not reach its top until fully a year later. Influenced much more by price-making forces than by value-making forces, Chrysler common in 1928 and 1929 followed a cycle all its own, conforming neither with the cyclical course of its group nor with that of the market as a whole.

Summed up in more general terms, then, there are three main types of long term fluctuation regarding which the common stock owner must constantly be on the alert, and which he must be constantly fitting into his plans and forecasts:

Fluctuation which conforms with the broad average, or cyclical movement.

Fluctuation influenced chiefly by conditions within a given industry and group of stocks, and which may or may not conform with the broad average.

Independent fluctuation, conforming neither with the main cyclical trend nor with the trend within a given industry.

Obviously, the satisfactory working through of a common stock investment program entails the capitalization of these regular and irregular long term fluctuations in their favorable aspects, and the avoidance of their penalties in their unfavorable aspects. (In the main, the favorable aspects of value or price fluctuations are upward movements, the unfavorable aspects, downward.)

There are numerous types of shorter term fluctuation which need not detain us.

2. THE CYCLICAL FLUCTUATION AS A MAJOR PRICE-VALUE HAZARD

Cyclical fluctuations are responsible for important changes not only in the intrinsic values of common stocks, but in their prices.

A diversified list of common stocks, carrying, say, a market value of $100,000 at the peak of the 1919 bull market, would have sold for $65,000 in mid-1921, at the trough of the subsequent bear market.

The same block of stocks (worth $65,000 at the bottom of the 1921 bear market) could have been sold for something like $230,000 at the peak of the bull movement which reached its crest in the autumn of 1929, but had been marked down to $106,000—*i.e.*, had declined $124,000 in market value—at the subsequent 1930 bear trough.

Thus, the investor's viewpoint toward his holdings must be a duplex one.

First, it must take into consideration the specific and individual situations in which he is a partner —*i.e.*, his common stocks as individual entities. (So much attention has already been given to the problems involved in the selection of the ideal individual common stock, or its first and second cousins, that further comment on this phase is not necessary for the moment.)

Second, the viewpoint must take into consideration the cyclical phenomena of business—those violent eruptions which from time to time play havoc horizontally with *the majority of* values, quite regardless of their merits as individuals.

Thus, assuming that the investor had been successful in choosing individual stocks which somewhere approached the ideal, his "ideal investment operation" would have been as follows:

He would have sold, at the peak of the 1919 bull market, stocks which fetched him $100,000 in cash.

This sum would have been held intact until the exact low of the 1920–1921 bear market was reached, and then would have been reinvested in stocks.

These, in turn, would have been sold at the exact peak of the 1921–1929 bull swing, at which point they would have fetched $230,000. With this sum, the investor again would have come into the market as a purchaser when the exact low of the 1929–1931 bear market was reached. (Whenever that might have been; see later.)

If the investor had merely held continuously throughout the period 1919–1931, or in other words if he had not taken advantage of the cyclical

[209]

fluctuations in values and prices which occurred, the stocks which were priced at $100,000 in 1919 would have been worth somewhere around $100,000 at the 1931 low. This would have been the capital sum with which the investor entered the *next* bull market, rather than the $230,000 with which he would have had to operate if he had ducked in and out of the market in synchronization with the cyclical swings.

In other words, from the standpoint of successful acquisitiveness, the idea would be to make progress on one's own account while the country as a whole was making progress, but to lie quiescent in the financial dugout while the penalties for too rapid progress, or progress that had been carried too far, were being paid.

Translated into the stock market situation, this would imply that the wise men and the fools would swap stocks back and forth between each other with a sort of pendulum-like regularity. At the top of each major bear market, the wise men would sell all the stocks to the fools, who would carry them down on the ensuing bear movement, and would finally become so embarrassed by the procedure that they would be obliged to sell back to the wise men, at the very bottom of the bear movement. Then the wise men would carry the stocks up again on the next major bull movement, sell out once more to the fools at the peak, at a handsome profit, and so on monotonously.

This, indeed, is the classical tradition as to how the thing is operated. The "pools," the "big "fellows," the "insiders," the "bank crowd," etc., are all supposed to sell their stocks to the "public," (*i.e.*, the foolish public) near the peaks of bull markets, and to buy them back again from the foolish public at much lower prices near the troughs of bear markets.

In all of Christendom there are few legends more untrustworthy.

If the program outlined above were actually practicable of fulfillment, it would be a program so ruthless, so selfish, so destructive, that it would be repugnant to any fair-minded person. To outline a long term investment program based primarily upon taking advantage of someone else's ignorance would be tantamount to counseling the advance of one's financial interest by cheat and fraud.

But no one's sensibilities need be offended in the slightest. The button-button-who's-got-the-button stock market program (wise man to fool, fool to wise man, then wise man to fool again, etc.) might conceivably be possible for a relatively small number of wise men, but it would be utterly impossible for any considerable percentage of the wise men's fraternity, for three very simple reasons:

[211]

1. The fools do not command enough purchasing power at the peaks of bull markets to enable them to take over the wise men's stock;

2. The wise men are not wise enough at bull-market peaks really to want the fools to take over their stock (*i.e.*, they are as foolish as the fools) and especially

3. The wise men are not wise enough to know when they should sell.

It is quite true that the "public" was caught in the stock market crash of 1929, and is similarly caught in every other market crisis. The chief reason it gets caught is because it is over-extended financially; is carrying heavier loans than it should. But rest assured that when it does get caught, it always has plenty of high-brow, long-pursed company.

Let us return, for a moment, to the 1929 crisis. During the two years preceding, virtually every important financial group in the country which had a security-distributing organization had organized its own investment trust. Certainly, those behind these investment trusts were the "big fellows" of our financial world—the "insiders," the members of the "bank crowd."

Had the investment trusts passed their common-stock holdings along to the fools when the 1929 peak in the stock market was reached? They had not. The great majority of them were virtually 100 per cent invested when the crash came, and either through choice or necessity they rode down the ensuing bear market still nursing most of their holdings, and losing a substantial percentage of their capital. The only proof of this statement that is necessary is a comparison of the equity values of the common stocks of the larger investment trusts, at the 1931 low and at the 1929 high.

Were the security-distributing organizations of the big commercial banks out of common stocks when the 1929 crash came? They were not. Their inventories were adequate—in some cases, so extremely adequate that substantial losses in capital had later to be publically acknowledged.

Were the industrial "insiders" out of common stocks when the last crisis arrived—the directors, presidents, vice-presidents, treasurers, and secretaries of our large industrial concerns, who are supposed to be able to do so well in the stock market because of the advance information they are in a position to obtain? They were not out of stocks, on the average. They were very much in stocks. Ask ten representative industrial executives and, if you get a truthful answer, you will learn that nine of the ten were carrying a full line of common stocks in September, 1929.

[213]

Some of the "big fellows" and "insiders" had passed their stocks along to others when the crash came; some of the "outsiders" had done the same thing. They were the lucky ones—a very, very small lucky minority. As a result of conversations with hundreds of individual investors during the past two years, conversations under circumstances which made it quite inadvisable and unnecessary for anyone to misrepresent actual facts, this writer feels absolutely safe in making the general statement that a preponderant majority of those who held common stocks in September, 1929, continued to hold in substantial volume throughout the major bear market of 1929–1931. Most of the selling that was done was either (*a*) occasioned by unreasoning fear and therefore the sold stocks were soon replaced, or (*b*) was made necessary by vanishing margins.

Hence much of the sympathy for the "sucker" who takes over the "big operator's" stock at the peaks of bull markets is wasted. It is physically impossible to transfer the certificates to the suckers, because they do not have enough money to make the purchase, if for no other reason, and those who according to the old legend should be busy selling out are, in reality, busy holding on, even acquiring more stock as the markets reach their peaks, and assuring themselves that the *new era* is here at last.

[214]

Cyclical phenomena are altogether democratic in the good and ill which they work in the stock market. The only reason the "little fellow" usually gets hurt worse than the "big fellow" in a market crash is because his financial resources are smaller, and he is customarily over-extended to a greater extent.

So it is obvious that cyclical fluctuations in the stock market constitute a hazard of major importance for those who carry common stocks in their investment portfolios. No investment policy can ignore this hazard. Successful investment policy must not only be conscious of cyclical fluctuations, must not only be able to recognize their extremes as they are approached, but must utilize them to its own purpose.

It will be maintained in what follows that, although it is never possible to identify the absolute peak of a major bull movement nor the absolute trough of a major bear movement, it should be possible to identify zones which signal the approaching climax of a bull movement, and likewise zones which signal the approaching bottom of a bear movement.

It will further be held that these zones should be utilized alternately to lighten ship on the one hand, and to take on additional investment cargo on the other hand.

[215]

Such a procedure, if it were followed by a sufficiently great number of informed investors, would not be inimical to the broader economic welfare; quite to the contrary, it would advance general economic welfare.

Cyclical fluctuations in business activity, major bear and bull markets on the stock exchanges, are without any doubt among the craziest, most destructive phenomena that a civilized society ever tolerated.

The idea that it is inevitable that we should overdo prosperity (get drunk on it) or that we should overdo depression (get hypnotized by it) is simply a childish, fatalistic idea.

Booms do not add anything real to a society's capital; what is added in the boom stage is canceled in the subsequent corrective decline. Depressions do not really chasten an industrious, ingenious people; they merely bring privation and want to millions of people who have done nothing in the world to deserve such treatment.

Frenzied stock markets do not add permanent wealth; it is mostly paper wealth, quickly canceled. Bear markets do not teach the masses of people to be conservative, thoughtful investors.

Economic progress is a matter of the development of natural resources, the development of technology, the development of consumer habits

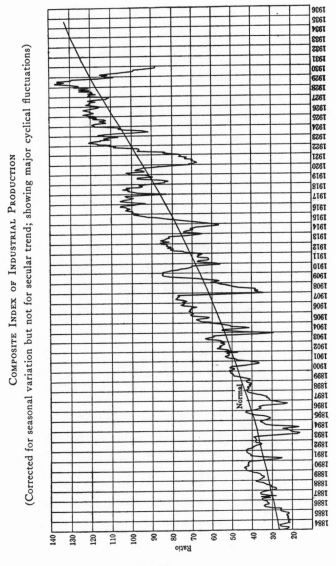

CHART 12

COMPOSITE INDEX OF INDUSTRIAL PRODUCTION

(Corrected for seasonal variation but not for secular trend; showing major cyclical fluctuations)

and of financial systems. There is no earthly reason why these things need go by fits and starts. They do go that way, of course, but that is a fact, rather than a reason. There is reason to believe that we could get farther with our progress program more rapidly if we could move more steadily.

Therefore, anything that can be done to shave off the peaks of booms and bull markets, and anything that can be done to fill up the valleys of business depressions and bear markets, *is well done —is done in the interests of public welfare, and will tend to advance public welfare.*

It takes money to engineer booms. Enterprisers cannot get money unless investors let them have it. Except in the frenzied final stages of a major bull market, investors customarily do not let enterprisers have more money than is good for them. This is merely another way of saying that new securities are much easier to float in a major bull market than at any other time.

Merely as one example, think for a moment what the result would be if a considerable number of informed and financially resourceful investors —say five to ten thousand of them—sold individual stocks of every description every time their yields dropped below 3½ per cent, and purchased the stocks that they wanted on the basis of careful analysis, whenever their yields crept above 6 to 7 per cent.

This would supply an automatic correction of market excesses. Both selling and buying would be spread over a period of time. As Stock X, paying $3.50 per share, crossed 100, it would be in sufficient supply to hold its price within reasonable limits. As it worked down toward 60–70, it would be in sufficient demand to prevent a price debacle.

Applied to a considerable number of stocks, over a period of time, the result of this kind of blind operation would assuredly be to flatten down the peaks of bull markets, and to build up the troughs of bear markets. We would get the same place in the long run—*i.e.*, upward to a higher plane of both values and prices—but would get there more steadily, and with fewer casualties.

I am certainly not advocating any such arbitrary method of investment practice. To do so would be something more than mere stupidity. But I am pointing out that a considerable body of informed investors, selling too soon on the basis of sound economic analysis, and buying too soon on the basis of the same kind of analysis, would provide the market with a stabilizing factor of remarkable force. The effects would be equally noticeable in general business activity.

[219]

Therefore, the furtherance of investment knowledge is not merely the advancement of the personal satisfaction of these informed investors, but, if such knowledge can be disseminated widely enough, it would undoubtedly result in enhanced stability in the markets. The long term upward fluctuation would be the same; the shorter movements would be less violent.

We shall return to this theme later on. But before doing so, we shall have a look at what evidence there existed, if any, to mark September 7, 1929, as the day of days in the greatest bull market in history. We shall likewise have a look at the significant events which occurred during the months immediately preceding September, 1929.

The purpose of such an inquiry is obvious: to locate such guideposts as we can, in the hope that they may be of help to us in the *next* crisis. We know that conditions vary radically from one crisis to the next; that the causes which underly each crisis are vastly different. But there are some situations which, economists have reason to conclude, are common to the majority of crises. These we shall be especially upon the alert to identify.

3. SEPTEMBER 7, 1929—THE DAY AND THE ZONE

September 7, 1929, is assumed to be the day on which the great 1921–1929 bull market reached its crest because the Standard Statistics Company's weighted average of the market values of ninety leading stocks registered its maximum high at that day's closing prices.

Other averages bear slightly different testimony, but the variance is only a matter of a few days, and is of slight consequence. One day, falling somewhere within the first fortnight of September, is as good as another. Each possessed its own characteristics, but no characteristics of outstanding importance.

September 7, 1929 (a Saturday) was a day of rapid recovery in the market—recovery from a technical reaction and from a bad case of nerves. Earlier in the week Mr. Roger W. Babson, the statistician, in a public address had made some very pointed remarks to the effect that stock prices were higher than they should be, that they deserved to sell lower, and that, as a matter of fact, they were likely, sometime, to sell lower.

The market acted like a boy caught stealing jam. It had a suspicion that Mr. Babson might be right, and it was fully as long as two or three days before that unwelcome suspicion had been entirely eradicated. It had, presumably, been entirely eliminated by the end of business on September 7; prices during the day's trading had risen smartly but not spectacularly; the volume of shares traded on the New York Stock Exchange amounted to 2,593,400. Neither the rapidity of the day's rise, nor the volume of trading, were record-breaking: there had been many days during the preceding six months upon which average prices had increased more rapidly; numerous Saturdays (Saturday is a two-hour trading day, as compared with five hours for a full day) upon which volume had been as heavy.

Let us turn for a moment to the financial pages of the careful and conservative *New York Times*, and see if we find there, either in the financial columns of September 7 or September 8, any suggestion whatsoever that September 7 *might* have been the last day of the greatest bull market in history.

In the issue of September 7 (and referring of course to the doings on September 6) this extraordinary analysis appeared under the heading: "Topics in Wall Street—News, Comment and

Incident on the Stock Exchange and in the Financial Markets."

Without hesitation, the stock market resumed the advance yesterday with vigor. Wall Street had generally expected that the market would at least temporarily be nervous and shaken yesterday. On the contrary, it opened with advances, and before the day was over had cancelled most of the losses of Thursday. The stock market community poured out scorn unstintingly on the oracle who, in the view taken yesterday, had "stampeded" Wall Street into a hasty liquidating movement. Stocks were taken in large blocks throughout the day at rising prices. Almost every active stock which participated in Thursday's break rose sharply yesterday. The net gains ranged from 2 to 10 points in the market leaders. Outwardly, Wall Street acted as if the $137,000,000 increase in brokers' loans announced on the afternoon before was a development of no importance.

IDENTIFYING THE BUYERS

Onlookers in Wall Street appeared to be convinced that stocks were going into "strong hands." The superior investment issues were bought in large quantities throughout the day, indicating that powerful financial groups were either making a demonstration or were picking up stocks at prices which were considered attractive. That investment trusts were in the market leading commission brokers admitted. Little odd-lot business was done. One house which ordinarily receives hundreds of odd-lot orders in a day reported yesterday that not more than twenty-five of the day's orders involved lots of fewer than 100 shares.

[223]

The Recovery a General One

It was not only on the New York Stock Exchange and the curb market that definite recovery took place yesterday, but in practically all other security markets. Trading over the counter resulted in generally higher prices, and according to reports received by brokers from the outlying exchanges, the wave of hysteria which swept the market on Thursday afternoon was short lived.

And under the same heading on September 8, the *Times* said:

Although the process of bidding up groups of "trading favorites" was repeated on the Stock Exchange yesterday, there was not the same enthusiasm which distinguished Friday's market. Many stocks made further sharp gains, but there were scattered declines and the last fifteen minutes of trading witnessed a lively selling movement. Taken altogether, the two-hour market was one of ill-distributed activities, with interest centered in fifteen or twenty "fast steppers." Wall Street's attitude as expressed in office discussions remained optimistic, and there was common talk of proposed "demonstrations" in the coming week.

In another column on September 8, under the headline "Stock Prices Rise to New High Levels," the *Times* declares:

With its losses of Thursday entirely cancelled, the stock market yesterday rounded out one of the most eventful weeks of the year by lifting itself into new high ground. During the two hours of trading on the New York Stock

[224]

Exchange 2,593,400 shares changed hands, which was at the rate of about 6,500,000 shares for a full five-hour day.

Yesterday's advance, while not as general as that of Friday, brought into the spotlight fifteen or twenty stocks upon which the market community seemed to be concentrating. In these issues the price swings were unusually wide, the final quotations disclosing net gains ranging from 3 to 16 points.

Anyone who could have read into these statements even the most veiled intimation that the end of the new era had arrived would indeed have merited a place among the seers and astrologers of Wall Street. As clearly as it is possible to make it, the suggestion throughout was that the financial god was back in his heaven, all was well again in Wall Street.

The man who had dared intimate in public that stocks might be too high, on the average, had received his just deserts; stock buyers had poured upon him "scorn unstintingly." "Strong hands" were reaching out to grasp the stocks that the fools were offering for sale. "Powerful financial groups either were making a demonstration, or were picking up stocks at prices which were considered attractive." The big fellows rather than the little ones had charge of the fireworks: "Little odd-lot buying was done."

[225]

Before turning aside from the subject, we may have a hurried look at the character of some of the other news which filled the financial section of the *Times* on September 7 and 8. Excerpts from headlines alone will be sufficiently suggestive:

"*Chain Stores Show Big Gain in August* . . . Thirty-four Report Average Rise of 34 Per Cent in Sales Over Year Ago."

"*Income of Railways Generally Increased* . . . Gains as Great as 72.5 Per Cent in Net Operating Receipts Made for Seven Months."

"*Record Year Seen for Canadian Mines* . . . Output in First Six Months Valued at $123,702,334, as against $105,632,571 in 1928."

"*Business Expected to Resume Its Pace* . . . Commercial Reviews Report a Temporary Restraint, but Say It Is About Ended."

"*Steel Ingot Output Large Last Month* . . . Operations Maintained at 93.3 Per Cent of Capacity, against 82.10 Per Cent in 1928 Period."

"*Chicago Banks Owe Little to Reserve* . . . Loans from Federal Institution Reduced in Year to $1,000,000 from $146,000,000."

"*Call Money Drops to 6 Per Cent Rate* . . . Bankers Ascribe Sudden Fall from 9 per cent to Liquidation in the Stock Market . . . *Other Factors Aid Credit.*"

"*Buying Features Unlisted Stocks* . . . Bank Shares Recover from the Declines of Thursday—Utility Groups Active."

"*New Highs Reached in Trading on Curb* . . . Standard Power and Light Leads Advance Which Carries Broad

[226]

List to Good Gains. Trading on the Curb Exchange yesterday resulted in numerous substantial gains, chiefly among the utilities, but at the same time there were scattered losses throughout the list. Oil issues also provided their share of support.

"*Wheat Advances, Bears Are Caught* . . . Those Who Sold Early Caused a Price Drop, but Values Quickly React."

"*Autumn Reviving Special Trade Lines* . . . Seasonal Acceleration Evident Despite Retarding Effects of Widespread Heat . . . *Industrial Centres Busy* . . . Reports from the Federal Reserve Districts Generally Favorable— Builders More Active."

Certainly in none of this news was there any warning that business was on the threshold of an important decline. The truth of the matter is that business had reached and passed its peak four months earlier. But this was not generally recognized. There was a general expectation that the forward movement would be resumed without unnecessary delay.

Thus it is quite too obvious to call for any further comment that there was no way in which any human being could have with any degree of assurance identified September 7, at that time, as the day that wrote finis beneath the great bull market of 1921–1929. A relatively small number of persons might have guessed it to be such. They could not have proved it to be so— at the time.

[227]

On the other hand, there was a redundancy of evidence that the several months preceding September 7, and the few weeks immediately succeeding, spanned a period of grave economic danger— a period in which careful, conservative investors should have been steadily reducing their holdings of common stocks. This evidence was not available in any single issue of any newspaper or financial publication: it was cumulative over a period of months: part of it inferential, but none the less clear.

Glance first at the evidences of financial strain which were so abundant:

1. For some unexplainable reason, the rate for call loans took a nose dive on September 6. It had been ruling at 9 per cent, but on that day dropped to 6 per cent. The average yield on dividend-paying stocks at the beginning of September, 1929, was about $3\frac{1}{2}$ per cent, it will be recalled. In other words, with call money costing even as little as 6 per cent, the average dividend paying common stock would just about pay half of its "keep."

2. The rate on time loans on stock exchange collateral, however, did not in early September reflect the weakness in call loans. The quoted rate for the first-named class of loans on September 7 was $8\frac{3}{4}$ to 9 per cent, as compared with $6\frac{1}{2}$ per cent a year earlier.

3. Outstanding credit of commercial banks had been expanding steadily for a long time. The first week in September, 1929, loans, discounts, and investments of Federal Reserve member banks stood above 22½ billions; 4½ per cent greater than at the beginning of 1928; 14 per cent greater that at the beginning of 1927; 36 per cent greater than at the beginning of 1924.

4. Loans of member banks on security collateral were at a new peak for all time. Amounting to 7.6 billions, they were 10½ per cent greater than at the beginning of 1928; 27½ per cent greater than at the beginning of 1927; 79 per cent greater than at the beginning of 1924.

5. Bank deposits, strange to say, were shrinking while bank loans were expanding. At 20 billions, total deposits of member banks were 3½ per cent less than they had been at the beginning of 1928. (Shrinking deposits in the face of rising loans usually constitute a financial warning signal.)

6. Brokers' loans were at a new peak. They amounted to 6.5 millions. Of this outstanding credit, loans "for the account of others," *i.e.*, for corporations, individuals, etc., amounted to 3.6 billions, or to about 56 per cent of the total. The loans of "others" had increased by 50 per cent since the beginning of 1929; by 168 per cent since the beginning of 1928.

[229]

Here was a clear and unmistakable danger signal. Not only was the signal given by the proportion of loans of "others" to the total amount of stock market credit extended on call, but likewise by the rapidity with which it had been growing.

And the peril that was forecast actually arrived. The "others" who loan their idle funds to the stock market feel no responsibility to the market whatsoever. Their money is there for one purpose, and for one purpose only: to suck, vampire-like, the last possible drop of profit. The reckless and unnecessary calling of the loans of "others" in October and November, 1929, contributed in important measure to the two successive market panics which occurred in those months.

7. Just one more financial reference: the rediscount rate at the New York Federal Reserve Bank had ruled at 5 per cent for more than a year prior to early August, 1929. On August 9, 1929, the rate was raised to 6 per cent. Now, anyone looking over the long term record of the rediscount rate at New York will promptly appreciate that 6 per cent is an abnormally high rate. Examination of the record will also show that a single upward step in the rate amounting to 1 full per cent is also a radical move. The usual practice is to advance or reduce the rate by stair steps of ½ per cent each.

[230]

Federal Reserve authorities have made the statement, in the hearing of this writer, that they believe they can break any bull market with a 6 per cent rediscount rate.

A relatively high call loan rate is not, in itself, necessarily the signal of an impending cyclical change in the stock market.

A high time loan rate is not in itself necessarily such a signal.

Steadily expanding commercial credit, constantly touching new peaks, is not necessarily in itself such a signal.

Falling bank deposits, in the face of expanding loans, do not, in themselves, necessarily constitute such a signal.

Brokers' loans at more than 6.5 billions, with more than half of this total supplied by irresponsible "others" do not, in themselves, necessarily constitute such a signal.

A 6 per-cent rediscount rate at New York does not necessarlly constitute such a signal.

But all of these signals taken together should quite clearly indicate to any careful observer that something extraordinary is occurring in the credit situation. Remember that stock prices can only continue to move forward as long as the credit available to security purchasers continues to expand. On a 6 per cent rediscount rate, a 6 to 9 per cent call rate, a 9 per cent time rate, and a brokers' loan structure which has already exhausted the surplus lending power of the commercial banks and is drawing more than half its supply of funds from individuals and corporations, there is certainly not much reason to believe that stock market credit can be expanded greatly farther.

The credit situation as a whole gave a clear warning to conservative investors in the summer and early autumn of 1929. Credit is one of the most vital forces in any bull market, and a credit strain will always constitute one of the major factors that will bring that market to its term. Watch the credit situation closely. Begin to get frightened too soon, rather than too late.

I. Begin to get frightened when you see the rediscount rate at New York anywhere above 5 per cent, and be particularly alarmed when you see it advanced one full point at a single jump.

II. Begin to get frightened when you see the cost of carrying stocks twice as great as the income return therefrom, and get more and more frightened as this spread increases.

III. Begin to get frightened when you see security owners borrowing more than 5 billions from their brokers. This cannot be a permanent debt; it must be settled, sometime, somehow. Moreover, not only is it a debt that must be paid, but it is a debt subject, for the most part, to cancellation at the will of the lenders—and have no doubt that the lenders will cancel whenever it suits their purpose to do so.

IV. Begin to get frightened when you cannot see where the additional money is coming from that will be needed if stock prices are to go still higher.

V. Begin to get frightened when you see the loans and investments of the Federal Reserve Member Banks above 20 to 21 billions, because you may be certain that, with all this credit outstanding, a considerable portion of it is being used unwisely.

All of the evidence now available suggests that the credit situation in the United States entered the danger zone about the middle of 1928—say a year, at the very least, before the stock market made its ultimate peak. *Imagine how much economic anguish would have been saved, how much real wealth would have been conserved, if a considerable body of informed investors had begun selling securities vigorously, and denying additional funds to enterprisers, in mid-1928.*

VI. Begin to get frightened when it becomes obvious that large groups of security holders are experiencing losses. This is a bad symptom for two reasons: (a) the losing holders become uneasy and are likely to take market action which may precipitate a crisis; and (b) more important still, they are often

[233]

obliged to press securities for sale, in an effort to protect their weakened positions.

Examples:

1. Despite the fact that "the market as a whole," or the average stock, in other words, did not reach its peak until early September, a number of important groups of stocks had been declining steadily for several months previous. These included the important automobile group, the fertilizer, drug, leather, textile, theatre, sugar, traction, coal, meat packing and automobile tire groups. Between January 1, 1929, and September 5 of that same year, the aggregate market values of the common stocks of 112 companies operating in these industries registered a net depreciation of more than 1¼ billion dollars—and this while the market as a whole was still moving upward at a feverish rate. The holders of these depreciating stocks were not only frightened, but were obliged to make an important volume of sales to cover shrinking margins.

2. High grade bonds had been falling in price. As a matter of fact, the bond market reached its peak in March, 1928, and fell steadily thereafter. The average high grade bond which could have been sold for $1,005 in March, 1928, fetched only $949 on September 7, 1929. This meant that the capital and surplus of commercial banks was

shrinking, because these institutions inevitably employ a considerable amount of their secondary reserve in the bond market.

3. High grade preferred stocks were also falling in price. The average gilt edge issue which would have sold for $135.30 in April, 1928 (the peak month) would have brought only $126.90 at the end of the first week in September, 1929.

4. Average stock prices on the London stock exchange reached a cyclical peak in the first quarter of 1929. Late in September, 1929, the lid blew off a British situation being engineered and guided by a frenzied financier named Clarence C. Hatry. When the crash came, claims against his various companies were well in excess of 10 million pounds sterling. A number of large scale British investors were badly hurt; others were badly frightened. There is now no doubt but that, immediately after the Hatry failure, certain British interests were obliged to dispose of significant blocks of American securities.

> *The jester doffed his cap and bells,*
> *And stood the mocking court before;*
> *They could not see the bitter smile*
> *Behind the painted grin he wore.*

The losses which holders of certain classes of common stocks, holders of high grade bonds and preferred stocks were taking, and the resultant anxiety, constituted the bitter smile behind the painted grin of the stock market's final merry spree.

VII. Begin to get frightened when business activity reaches a tempo which cannot be sustained unless the old norms of performance are to be abandoned.

Examples:

1. The Standard Statistics Company's index of aggregate industrial production averaged 12 per cent greater than computed normal during the first nine months of 1929.

2. The Federal Reserve Bank of New York's index of the total volume of trade also averaged 12 per cent greater than normal during the same period.

3. The same institution's clearings index of business averaged 11 per cent greater than normal during the same period.

4. Production of automobiles in the United States and Canada during the first nine months of 1929 was respectively 33 per cent, 58 per cent, and 31 per cent greater than in the corresponding periods of 1928, 1927, and 1926.

5. Production of steel ingots during the first nine months of 1929 was respectively 17 per cent, 28 per cent, and 21 per cent greater than in the corresponding periods of 1928, 1927, and 1926.

6. Imports during the first nine months of 1929 were 13 per cent greater and exports 8 per cent greater, than in the corresponding period a year earlier.

Reference to the chart depicting the long term trend of the volume of production, on page 217 preceding, will instantly suggest that there are few things in our economic organization as stable as the *rate* of growth of our general business activity, and at the same time few things as unstable as the *actual* growth. A change of as much as 8 to 10 per cent in business activity, from one year to another, is a very radical change indeed. Such a change is usually accompanied by blithering chatter about the arrival of the *new era*, but never in the past has the long term trend line of business registered a change of any such magnitude. *It is the fluctuations about the trend line that show the changes. The trend line itself moves steadily, slowly.*

A swing of business to an abnormal level cannot conceivably be maintained at that level unless the normal, or trend line, has also been stepped suddenly and permanently upward. As previously stated, this has never yet occurred. Persistence of general business activity in a high zone of supra-normality for any period of months is inevitably a danger signal, because it forecasts a subsequent stepping down from this untenable level, and for

[237]

business the stepping down process is always painful.

VIII. Begin to get frightened when either automobile production or new building activity appears to have developed a definite downward trend. As our present economy is organized, these two tails wag the American business dog. Either or both of them, operating at a supra-normal level, can make a business boom. Either or both of them, declining sharply, can cause enough disturbance to break the backbone of a boom.

The automobile industry had not given a decisive signal of distress by September, 1929. The trend of output was downward, at a rate more rapid than the normal seasonal one. But the pace of decline had not yet become alarming, and spring output had been so thoroughly supra-normal that a considerable sliding off in output was generally accepted as reasonable.

Building, however, gave two very clear signals of distress: one from the volume side, and one from the financial side.

New construction in the United States reached the peak of a long upward movement in April, 1928, and thereafter declined steadily. New contracts let in September, 1929, were smaller than in any other September since 1924; they amounted to only 64 per cent of those let in the 1928 peak month (square-foot basis).

Bear in mind that the decline from the 1928 peak had been relatively steady; anyone who had taken the trouble to have looked at the figures could not possibly have missed its significance as a cyclical phenomenon. There was also evidence that surplus capacity, especially in residential and office space, was being completed and coming on to the market at a rapid rate.

On the financial side, so many real estate bonds had worked into an unfavorable position by early autumn, 1929, that this source of new building capital had practically dried up. Moreover, mortgage money of all kinds was becoming progressively more difficult to obtain. Second mortgage money was commanding a high premium. First mortgage money in some districts was virtually unobtainable. These circumstances taken together clearly forecast a further decline in building activity during the winter of 1929–1930 and in the spring of the last-named year.

IX. Begin to get frightened when, in a period of seemingly widely diffused general prosperity, commodity prices persist in following a steadily downward course. This is normally a symptom of an oversupply of goods, and forecasts both a decline in the margin

[239]

of profit of certain kinds of producers, and that these producers are getting hurt—and worried.

Bradstreet's index reached the peak of an upward cyclical movement in January, 1928, and thereafter declined, quite gently, but equally insistently.

The September, 1929, index was some 6 per cent below its 1928 peak. Several very important commodities had been declining quite violently. The average price of silver in September, 1929, was 15 per cent less than at the 1928 peak. (Silver is generally considered not only a very sensitive commodity, being subject to world-wide influence, but likewise one the movements of which have important barometric significance.) Crude rubber was down 49 per cent from the 1928 peak in September, 1929; wheat was down 29 per cent.

X. Begin to get frightened when, in a period of seemingly widely diffused general prosperity, the people of important geographic sections are having their purchasing power curtailed.

There was ample evidence in mid-1929 that the purchasing power of our farming communities, and of various of our important foreign markets, was seriously out of balance with out industrial and Wall Street purchasing power.

XI. Begin to get frightened when stock prices rise much faster than earnings.

Such calculations are always rather indefinite, but the available data indicate that during the second and third quarters of 1929, average stock prices were leaping upward at a rate about *twice* as rapid as the rate of gain in corporation profits.

XII. Begin to get frightened when new financing looks as though it were getting out of hand.

In the first place, abnormally heavy financing puts a strain on the money markets: the new securities can be absorbed only if old securities are forced for sale, or if bank loans are greatly increased.

In the second place, abnormally heavy new financing indicates that investors are becoming reckless with their capital, and gives grounds for the suspicion that at least a sizable portion of the money which is being shoveled in so easily is likely to be recklessly employed.

According to the data compiled by the Standard Statistics Company, new corporate security issues during the first nine months of 1929 amounted to 9,580 million dollars. This compared with the sums raised in like periods of preceding years as follows:

29 per cent greater than in 1928
47 per cent greater than in 1927
95 per cent greater than in 1926
104 per cent greater than in 1925
176 per cent greater than in 1924

XIII. Begin to get frightened when the public shows a willingness to pay from a dollar and a quarter to a couple of dollars each for one dollar bills.

Late in July, 1929, the common stock of the Shenandoah Corporation (the second of the Goldman Sachs large investment trusts) was offered to the public at $17.50 per share. Five million shares of this stock were sold with apparently about as much ease as that with which the average investor takes down the receiver of his telephone and instructs his broker to purchase 10 shares of United States Steel Corporation common stock.

Offered late in July at 17½, this stock on August 13 closed on the New York Curb 35½— or at a premium of about 103 per cent. At its offering price the stock must have carried some "loading," to cover selling costs. The premium over actual value, that is, must have amounted to at least 105 per cent. In other words, for a Shenandoah Corcorporation one dollar bill the public was willing to pay somewhere around $2.05 about three weeks after it had been offered for sale.

Now, actual value could not conceivably have increased at any such rate. The public was beginning to believe in magic. It was willing to pay great premiums for the privilege of having someone else invest its money.

[242]

This is an extreme example, and is cited, of course, without any suggestion of criticism against the offering corporation. A wild public had the bit in its teeth, and simply could not be restrained in any reasonable fashion. The common stock of Goldman Sachs Trading Corp. sold at a premium of 20 per cent within a month after it had been offered; Blue Ridge at a premium of 37 per cent; Lehman Corporation at a premium of 32 per cent; Tri-Continental at a premium of 17 per cent; etc.

The list of "watch your steps" might be indefinitely extended, but without greatly advancing the argument. As previously suggested, the dominating influences at the peak of one given prosperity cycle are always different from those observable at the peak of any other cycle. Hard-and-fast rules of identification cannot be drawn. The factors just referred to are usually present in one form or another, although sometimes they are so well disguised that their identification becomes extremely difficult.

The point of outstanding importance is that in every prosperity cycle, as it reaches its peak, there are numerous evidences of situations which should cause uneasiness to the conservative investor. He is not helpless against such situations. All he needs to do is to keep his eyes open and to be constantly studying, checking, rechecking, forecasting, reforecasting.

Summary—Investment Policy

1. *It is a human impossibility for the business or stock market analyst to identify, at the time, the exact peak of either an expanding period of prosperity in business, or of a major bull movement in the stock market.*

2. *It is* NOT *impossible to identify danger zones, extending, say, over a period of several months. Indeed, investment policy which does not take into adequate account the significance of these danger zones cannot hope to get very far.*

3. *These zones should be utilized for the building up of cash reserves (or their equivalent); for the weeding out of the portfolio of issues of dubious merit; for the adjustment of credit obligations to a safe and sane basis; generally, for retrenchment and for getting one's investment house in order to weather a possible storm.*

Observe that no such specious advice as "Sell all stocks as a bull market approaches its crest," is given.

The reasons are very practical ones. In the first place, as previously pointed out, it would be a physical impossibility for the investment public to sell all of its stocks, because there would be no one to buy them, and no money with which to pay for them. It would even be physically impossible for the wise men to sell out to the fools as the climax drew near—or at any other time.

In the second place, in a country such as this one, where the long term trend of economic development is an upward trend, where the bulls have the best of the argument about two years out of three, or perhaps even three years out of four, on the average, not one investor out of a hundred, perhaps not even one out of five hundred, will ever believe, fully and whole-heartedly, that the end of a period of expansion actually is at hand.

As he sees unpleasant things developing he will find some way to laugh them off—some way to excuse them. He will find some reason why these factors might portend dangers at other times, but are impotent of ill at this particular time. He will forget what has happened in all periods of supranormal expansion in the past, and will find some reason for believing that *this* period is the one that is never going to crack.

Therefore, the investment public *cannot* get rid of its common stocks as a major bull market swings upward to its maximum level, *and probably would not get out of them if it could.*

The only hopes here expressed are (*a*) that as investment knowledge is slowly but surely more widely disseminated, more and more investors will take cognizance of the relationship between business, finance, and the stock market; (*b*) that they will more and more frequently identify periods of time in which it is wise to be steadily selling stocks; (*c*) that such selling will result in the conservation of a considerable amount of capital; and (*d*) that, if it occurs on a sufficiently great scale, it will actually prove a stabilizing force in the market, leveling off the peaks and raising the floor elevation of the valleys.

Specifically, a selling zone, a zone when conservatism should have been on the increase with the average investor, was clearly indicated from, say, May 1, 1929, to October 15, 1929.

Starting this 5½ month danger period at 206, the Standard Statistics Company's daily index of ninety stocks had risen to 254 on September 7, and was down to 240 on October 15. Sale of any important volume of stock early in the danger period would, then, have involved the loss of substantial *possible* profits. The investor who actually sold, and saw the market move steadily upward for several months thereafter, would have felt very bad about the loss of these *possible* profits. If he had made his sales on someone else's advice—that of his banker, his broker, or an economic service to which he subscribed—his bitterness

[246]

would have lost no time in registering itself in a formal letter of complaint.

He might have felt just a little bit better about the situation on November 13, 1929, however; on that day, the stock price index stood at 140.

4. THE 1930–1931 DEPRESSION ZONE

When this chapter was first written (early in 1931) it was done as a companion piece to the one immediately preceding and was appropriately labeled "December 16, 1930—The Day and the Zone." The tentative assumption was that the bear market which began in early September, 1929, had made its ultimate bottom when the low prices of December 16, 1930, were touched.

As the manuscript is revised (June, 1931) average stock prices, according to the Standard Statistics Company's index of ninety stocks, are at least 15 per cent lower than they were at the 1930 nadir. New lows have been succeeding each other with the regularity of new days. Darkness lies upon the face of the earth. The heart of man is sorely tried; his head bowed down. Business and security market courage have flitted away into the encircling gloom. No one knows, no one thinks it worth while to attempt to guess, whether the low points touched by the market in early June, 1931, will stand as the ultimate lows for the 1929–1931 major bear movement.

And, as a matter of fact, it makes virtually no difference, for the purposes of this study, as to whether the maximum bear point was touched December 16, 1930, or June 2, 1931, or will be touched December 15, 1931, or, for that matter, July 1, 1932. Here our concern is chiefly with the broader principles; the statistical facts, whatever they may be, are useful chiefly for illustration and example.

Standing at the beginning of the summer of 1931, and viewing the long decline in stock prices in retrospect, one fact emerges with singular clarity, viz.:

The ideal stock market operation during this period would have been to have sold all of one's common stocks on September 7, 1929, and to have kept one's money in the savings banks, or in Liberty bonds, *at least* until June, 2, 1931, or, if later, until the exact bottom of the major bear swing was reached; then to have repurchased to the full extent of one's resources, and to have reaped the maximum of golden harvest as the next major up-swing progressed.

Any other operation (except of course the short position, which can never be an investment position, and which is here entirely eliminated from consideration) would have been obviously wrong in the short term viewpoint.

It has already been observed that the gulf which lies between the ideal investment operation and the

[249]

practical one is of vast dimensions. In this particular case, it is of almost illimitable dimensions.
For the average investor, the ideal operation on the
way down was impossible—as it had been impossible previously on the way up—because there was
nothing to identify positively the exact bottom of
the market any more than there had been anything
to identify the exact top; because it is physically
impossible for the investment public as a whole to
sell its stocks at the peaks of cyclical movements
and reenter the markets at their troughs; and
because at such peaks and bottoms there is nothing
sufficiently convincing in the economic facts then
available to dictate, with assurance, the wisdom
or safety of such daring operations.

There is of course plenty in retrospect to demonstrate that the policy of absentation would have
been the wise one throughout the 1929–1931
decline. But as we go along with a security market
program from day to day, we must be viewing it
more in prospect than in retrospect. We must be
struggling continuously with tomorrow's probabilities, and make today's decisions on the basis of
reasonable projections.

Lessons are of course to be learned from hind-
sight. Policies are based upon experience. In this
section, therefore, we propose not merely to look
backward and point out what an intelligent com-

mon stock investor *should* have done during the 1929–1931 major bear market, but to try to sketch a reasonable outline of what he *would* have done . . . of what, on the basis of his knowledge at the time he took each important action, he would have felt more or less *justified* in doing.

Parenthetically, it may be said that this outline is not altogether hypothetical, nor even largely so. It constitutes a formally diagrammatized report of the composite investment experience of a considerable number of business-men investors with whose affairs this writer chances to have been familiar.

And be it repeated that, viewed from the date point of early June, 1931, most of the moves made by our so-called average, or typical investor would have been wrong—wrong as viewed from that date point, *but not necessarily and not probably wrong if re-viewed from the date point of, say, January 1, 1933.*

The penalties of carrying SOME *common stocks through a major bear movement must be regarded as among the normal hazards of a long term common stock investment program.* All investors *cannot* sell. So long as the human mind remains the same as it is, and so long as American economic psychology remains the same as it is, only a relatively small proportion of them *will* sell unless they are forced to do so.

[251]

We consider it of the utmost significance to note that the hazard of declining values and prices coincident with a cyclical drop in general business activity is one which attaches not merely to that section of the business structure which is represented by marketable securities, *but to virtually all branches of business enterprise.* Publicly owned business, privately owned fractional partnerships, and singly owned enterprises are subject to the same broad, devastating influences. (Further reference to this point will be made in the final section of this essay.)

To make the program which is to be outlined in the following paragraphs have any sense or meaning at all, it must be assumed that the hypothetical investor whose maneuvers we shall be examining found himself, after the smoke had cleared away from the stock market panic which ended November 13, 1929, with some actual cash in his possession. Of course he had depreciated securities—plenty of them. But we must assume that he had either been smart enough to cash *some* profits at the 1929 danger zone level, or had been frightened or forced into doing so by the October and November panics. In any event, he had some real money—spendable money.

His problem is twofold: (*a*) not to spend too soon, and (*b*) to come out of the 1930–1931 depression

CHART 13

STOCK PRICE INDEX OF NINETY ACTIVE STOCKS
(With indications of hypothetical buying and selling zones)

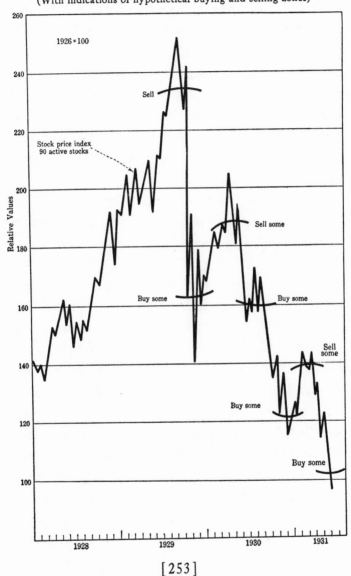

[253]

with the common stock portion of his fund practically 100 per cent invested.

He realizes that he faces a situation which is unpredictable in its details, even though it may be estimated in broad outline. He is wise enough to resolve to make haste slowly. He has just been through a harrowing experience. The new era has been knocked into a cocked hat. Our investor has been frightened back to fundamentals, and he is going to be very, very cautious—as properly he should be.

This course would have been justified, we believe, on the basis of facts as they were knowable at each step:

A. Our investor undoubtedly would have purchased *some* stocks during the last two weeks of November and the early part of December, 1929.

This would have been his first, and most costly, mistake. It would have been a gross mistake, viewed in retrospect from the first of June, 1931.

It would be silly to assume that our investor purchased any considerable quantity of stocks at the absolute 1929 low. Instead, let us assume that he made moderate purchases at, say, the mean price registered between November 13 and December 15, 1929. On the Standard Statistics Company's daily average of ninety leading stocks, the mean

[254]

price for this period of approximately one month following the November 13 low was 157. On June 1, 1931, average common stock prices (according to the report of this same index) were 65 per cent of their November 13, 1929, value.

As we have said, purchases on this basis, if they had been held continuously thereafter, would have proved a gross mistake. They need not, however, have constituted a *disastrous* mistake, if our investor had purchased moderately, as he should have done, and if he had purchased outright rather than on margin. We will assume that he did so, and that he kept a firm hand on the balance of his cash—the balance in this case being also the *majority* of his cash.

His two chief reasons for purchasing anything at all during, say, the first month following the November, 1929, panic, were:

1. Average prices were low *relatively*. As indicated by the movement of the indexes, the average stock which sold at index 254 on September 7 closed at 140 on November 13, or at 45 per cent of its recent peak price. The November 13-December 15 mean price was only 17 points above the November 13 minimum. This was certainly a price situation that was on its face tempting to even a conservative investor. Consideration of value could be hurled out of the window. Price

[255]

alone was attractive, in view of the vast decline which had occurred during the past month, and on the basis of economic facts that were then knowable.

2. It was not known how grave the ensuing business depression would be, and the prices that were quoted during late November and early December looked reasonable, even allowing for the worst probable subsequent developments in business. (Habits of the human race change very slowly; habits of thought, systems of estimation, developed in a period of long business boom simply cannot be erased in such a short space as a few months.)

Our investor's reasons for not buying *too* heavily immediately after the second 1929 panic would have been:

1. He knew no good reason why there should not have been a third stock market panic, and perhaps even a fourth.

2. He had no way of estimating the precise degree in which business would subsequently reflect what had already occurred on the stock market.

B. Our investor would have grown very uneasy in April and May, 1930.

Average prices had moved upward from index 140 in mid-November to index 206 on April 10—

[256]

a recovery of 66 points, or of 45 cents in the dollar.

But business had not shown the recovery that had been promised. In fact, it had shown disappointingly mild recovery—and this mostly of a seasonal character. Our investor would have sold some of his stocks in April and May, 1930—say at an average price somewhere around 195, which is a bit less than the mean price for those two months—because he would have become fearful that the cyclical improvement he had been expecting in business was not going to develop.

C. He would have bought some stock in June, July, and August, 1930, because:

1. The market was displaying a tendency to stabilize at that time somewhere around the level of 160.

2. There was reason to expect that real recovery in business would begin in the fall of 1930.

3. Business at that time looked rather thoroughly liquidated. Production and the volume of trade were at subnormal levels, as contrasted with supra-normal levels at the 1929 peak; interest rates were low; available credit was abundant; commodity prices were measurably lower than in 1929; everything, in a word, was dismal and "flat on its back."

[257]

4. Consultation of any statistical series would have demonstrated a wholly subnormal situation. If the investor held the theory that the long term trend of business activity was upward (refer to Chart 12 accompanying) he had no doubt that business would ultimately return to the normal trend line, then rise above it, as it always has done in the past. He would not have cared much whether it went a bit lower before it started upward. The big point was that *ultimately* an upward swing from a subnormal level was inevitable, if the observation of the past was to be the experience of the future.

5. But in view of the many uncertainties involved as to the time of the actual beginning of real recovery, our investor would by no means have risked *all* his remaining free capital on his judgment in June, July, and August, 1930. He would have bought moderately, and still retained an ample cash reserve against unknown contingencies.

And wisely so. In late August, in September, and in October, it became evident that the 1930 drought had caused much graver damage in the agricultural regions than had been expected; important commercial banks began closing up like flees dropping off a dog's back; finally it dawned upon the minds of investors that there was to be no autumn recovery in general business activity. The depression was to deepen further. The stock market, which had been above index 170 in both July and August, moved downward to index 115 in mid-December.

D. Our investor would have bought some more stocks in December, 1930–January, 1931, for the same reason that he bought some in June, July, and August.

In the earlier period, business had appeared deflated; it appeared considerably *more* deflated in December and January. Prices were measurably lower. There was basis for the expectation that real recovery in business would start in the spring of 1931. Yields on good stocks were attractive. Money with which to carry stocks was not only plentiful, but cheap. All that was needed to stimulate the courage to buy stocks was confidence in the premise that the long term trend of business was upward, and that gross subnormalities had always, in the past, been corrected by a movement first back to normality and then forward into a zone of supra-normality.

But still the careful investor would have bought moderately. He would not yet have risked all of his reserve. The truth of the matter is that in December, 1930, and January, 1931, his chief basis for buying was (*a*) hope and (*b*) long term historical performance. There was virtually no concrete evidence that business recovery was at hand.

While there were reasons to assume that a spring bulge in activity was in prospect, and that we were scraping along on the bottom of the depression, there were at the same time grounds for fear that the spring fillip might not be sustained; that corporation earnings for the first half of 1931 might be shockingly scant; that the drought in the agricultural regions might persist through the 1931 crop campaign.

Our wise investor therefore resolved still to retain a substantial proportion of his cash until the situation was further clarified.

On the one hand, he wanted to be in a position to make additional purchases, purely on a price basis, if periods of important weakness should appear in the market.

On the other hand, he did not want to exhaust his reserve until he had something more than theory and hope upon which to proceed. He wanted to save a sizable sum until he saw real evidence of business improvement.

The most important point in any careful investor's program was the handling of his reserve. He would have been wholly defeated in his purpose if he had exhausted these reserves in November–

December, 1929; if he had exhausted them in June, July, and August, 1930, or in December, 1930–January, 1931.

E. Our investor would have sold some of his stocks in February and March, 1931.

He would have sold them chiefly for the reasons that prompted him to moderation in his last period of accumulation—because the fears that had dictated his earlier moderation were beginning to be realized.

Another expected spring bulge in business was petering out, having fallen far short of its expected possibilities. Business profits were not merely bad— they were terrible. Dividend rates were racing with one another to see which could slide the farthest down hill, and the most rapidly.

Commodity prices were failing to show the expected stabilization. More banking trouble was developing. The foreign bond market was exhibiting a menacing aspect, with several important repudiations threatened.

In a word, the good things that had been expected—logically—to arrive coincident with the opening of the buds on the trees in the early spring of 1931 simply did not come; many of the ill things that had been vaguely feared *did* come. The signal to lighten ship was rather clear and insistent, and many prudent investors took the hint.

F. Our investor would have replaced his February–March, 1931, sales sometime in the early summer of 1931 (say during the period May 15–July 1) and probably would have taken an even more aggressive stand.

Indeed, he probably would not only have replaced his earlier sales, but he would have spent additional cash; not all of his reserve even yet, of course, because he was still saving a sizable portion of it to lay out when he was reasonably sure that the business depression had *actually* reached its term. Stock prices would be higher when it was really known that the end had come, of course, but the insurance would be worth the money.

No adequate purpose would be served in going over again the story as to why a careful common stock investor would have felt justified in making substantial purchases in May–June, 1931. It is the same story as has previously been told, *only more so.* Stock prices were lower, and yields higher, than in what had been considered the preceding favorable buying periods. Taken as a whole, the business news was so bad that it could not conceivably get a great deal worse.

Business had not actually turned for the better, so far as was known, but it appeared to be well stabilized at a level somewhere near the low point that had been touched in December, 1930. Important readjustments in corporation costs were known to have been effected, which would show up in operating profits later on. Money was excessively cheap. There was the hope, and indeed the reasonable prospect, that the normal seasonal influences which would begin to exert themselves in the late summer and early autumn would give the impetus which would mark the slow, faint beginning of long term cyclical recovery.

Based upon the information which is available as this study goes to press, the stock buying carried out by our hypothetical investor in May–June, 1931, would have been altogether justified. It makes not the slightest difference whether still later developments may demonstrate it to have been unjustified; makes not the slightest difference, so far as the present argument is concerned, whether several additional buying and selling zones develop before the next major bull market gets under way.

In either event, the basic principles remain the same. These principles will be dealt with more in detail in the concluding pages of this section.

Before passing to them, however, it may be worth while to observe how, throughout a period of depression as well as through a period of prosperity, the pressure against the investor is preponderately on the side of optimism, *i.e.*, on the buying side.

Let us take, for example, the year ending June 1, 1931. The first seven months of this year, virtually all of the commonly used business indexes report, were characterized by a steady and rapid fall in general business activity. During the last five months of this period, activity was roughly stabilized at a point near the low level which had been touched in December, 1930. Throughout the entire period the dominating trend of common stock prices was downward. On June 1, 1931, no conservative student of conditions would have been willing to state that the 1930–1931 depression was yet over, or that common stock prices were ready to begin a major advance.

The alternate hope and despair during this depression was a matter of such importance that it splashed over from the financial sections of the daily newspapers (to which it is usually confined) and not infrequently exhibited itself on the front pages of these papers.

Not unexpectedly or unaccountably, hope exhibited itself much more often on the front page

[264]

news stories than did despair. That is to say, the bull point of view was much more in evidence, in the news columns of important and influential daily newspapers, than was the bear point of view. *The implication to buy securities was more frequent than the warning to sell.*

Take, merely as an example, the business and financial news which appeared on the front page of the *New York Herald Tribune* during the depression year ending June 1, 1931. Doubtless any other large city newspaper would have shown the same type of reports. The *Herald Tribune* files were used merely because they were convenient.

In setting forth the following data, there is not the slightest thought of criticism. In fact, quite the contrary. Public psychology would certainly not have been improved or ameliorated in the slightest if our daily newspapers had kept telling their readers how sick business and the stock market actually were. *The material that is reproduced here is chosen solely with the thought of further emphasizing our viewpoint that the average common stock investor would, at various times during the 1930–1931 depression, have made additional purchases of common stocks, and that he would have found it not at all difficult to have justified these purchases by the information which was being constantly made available to him.*

[265]

During the year ending June 1, 1931, the *New York Herald Tribune* printed, on its front page, eight stories referring directly in their headlines to bad business conditions or falling stock prices. These headlines were as follows:

October 1, 1930

Exchange Bars J. A. Sisto & Co.; Stocks Go Lower
Prices Drop after Brokerage Firm Is Forced into Suspension as Insolvent.

October 7, 1930

Exchange Calls Brokers on Bear Trading Reports
Business Committee Acts on Low Prices Tactics; Stocks Fall 3–18 Points.

October 10, 1930

Prince & Whitely Suspended as Market Breaks
Bankruptcy Petition Filed against Brokers; Stocks Drop from 3 to 10 Points.

October 15, 1930

Stock Exchange Heads Talk Stock Drop With Mr. Hoover
Whitney and Lindley Visit President at White House; Short Tactics Discussed.

March 30, 1931

Cunard's Net Profit Is Cut to $93,005
1930 Earnings Compare with $4,048,195 in 1929.

[266]

April 30, 1931

U. S. Steel Falls to 115 in Bear Raid on Stocks
Loses 9½ Points in Wave of Professional Selling That
Sets New Lows

May 4, 1931

Rail and Ferry Riders Decrease 13 Million Here
Transit Commission Finds Depression Cuts Fares to
387,199,613 in 1930

May 23, 1931

Farrell Sees Ruin in Steel Price Cutting
Bluntly Scoffs at Schwab Optimism at Institute; Says
Wages Are Being Cut in "Pretty Cheap Business"
Doubts Trade Earns Preferred Dividends
"Situation Is Diabolical" He Tells 1,000 Leaders; Hints
at Shut-Down.

Following are more than a score of the *Herald
Tribune's* front page headlines, printed during this
same period, referring either to rising stock prices,
favorable business factors, or the hope of prompt
business recovery. A number of others in the
same category have been omitted.

July 1, 1930

President Lauds Aid of States in Trade Recovery
$1,700,000,000 Building Plan "Balance Wheel" He Tells
Governors by Radio.

July 30, 1930

U. S. Steel Looks for Early Gains in Nation's Trade
Reports Earnings of $3.02 a Share Last Quarter with
Operations 63 P. C.

[267]

July 31, 1930

Ford Optimistic on Business as He Reaches 67

"It Will Be All Right" He Says During Visit at West Orange to Greet Edison Scholars.

August 8, 1930

World Business Revival Nearing, Barnes Asserts

Spur of Confidence Alone Is Found Needed as Signal for End of Depression

August 27, 1930

A. F. of L. Study Finds Increase in Employment

Green's Statement Cites ⅗0–1 P. C. Loss in Idle Ranks as Omen of Revival

September 17, 1930

President Finds Gain in Exports Bolsters Trade

$38,000,000 Increase over Preceding Month Held to Reflect Trend to Normal

October 3, 1930

President Calls Bankers to Speed Trade Revival; Finds Confidence Gains

Economic Readjustment Far Along, Requires Extension of Credit to Complete Recovery, He Says

October 11, 1930

Stocks Recovery after 415 Sink to Record Lows

Steel Up 3⅛ in Rally on 6,296,918-Share Day; Bargain Hunters Buying

October 15, 1930

Bears Curbed in Borrowing, Stocks Rally

Greatest Lack of Loanable Issues in History of Market

Threatens to End Activity of Shorts
Compelled to Pay Premium for Steel.
Situation Believed the Result of Exchange Campaign
against Raiders.

October 23, 1930

Industrial Chiefs in Session Seek Trade Stabilizer
Business Ills Diagnosed and Remedies Offered at Chicago
U. Conference

October 27, 1930

Quickened Pace in Trade Found by World Survey
President's Conference Lists Raw Materials Demands;
Big Gain in N. Y. Savings

November 26, 1930

Standard Oils' Dividends for Year a Record
$286,666,728 Payments to Stockholders Exceed by
$17,020,801 Any Total Ever Set by Firms
Jersey Unit Paying Holders $50,000,000
Not One Default in Main Group; Extras Declared by
Many Subsidiaries

December 18, 1930

Stocks Rebound in Sharp Rally; Wheat Turns Up
Holiday and Bank Bonuses and Turn in Steel Trade
Rout Gloom in Wall Street

December 24, 1930

Reserve Rate Cut to 2% Here as Trade Tonic
Record Low Credit Level Set as Gesture of Confidence in
Soundness of Banks

December 31, 1930

Rail Issues Mount 1 to 6 Points; Other Stocks Rise in Sympathy

Market Experiences Its Biggest Day in Months after President's Announcement of Agreement on Eastern Railroad Consolidation Plan

January 1, 1931

500 Millions to Be Spent on Rail Plan

Roads in Merger Consider Projects to Give Two Lines Direct Access to New York

January 7, 1931

Motor Trades Future Hailed by President

Mr. Hoover Telephones His Greetings to Diners Here, Voicing Optimistic Note and Praising Program

Car Output Called Prosperity Index

Barnes Urges Government and Business Unite to Re-establish Confidence

January 31, 1931

All Jobs Secure, Big Industries Assure 500,000

Pledge of No Lay-offs by 25 Firms Held as Indicating Early Rout of Depression

February 7, 1931

Stocks Gain 3 Billion in Value in January

Advance 1st Since Last March; Brokers Loans Set a Low

February 10, 1931

Stock Prices Up 2–18 Points; 271 at High for Year

4,114,055 Shares Traded in Most Active Bull Session in Year; Auburn Leads Rise

February 11, 1931

Wall St. Hails Rise in Stocks as Bear Rout
Security Advance Continues amid Excitement on
Exchanges and Wheat, Copper and Cotton Gain
Specialty Bull Pools Run in the Shorts
4,762,625 Share Turnover Sees 276 New Highs and
Trading in 827 Issues

February 12, 1931

Market Moves Higher in Face of Profit Taking
Rise in Copper and Silver and Better Steel News Aid Wall
Street Bull Swing

March 2, 1931

Trade Upturn Is World-Wide, Barnes Reveals
U. S. Industry, Adjusted at Last, Has New Stimulant in
Spring Buying, He Says

April 30, 1931

Time Healing Business Ills, Says Lamont
Secretary Tells Chamber Readjustment Is Proceeding
Slowly; Maintaining Wages Praised

May 22, 1931

Program to Revive World's Prosperity Adopted at
Geneva
Definite Measures Taken by Subcommittees for Co-oper-
ation to Combat Present Economic Crisis
Study Parley Closes after 7-Day Session
International Agriculture Mortgage Credit Pact Is
Signed; Henderson Urges Cautious Progress

[271]

May 27, 1931

Trade Signals Point to Gain, White House Study Shows
Administration Retaining Attitude of Caution, Discloses
   Better Conditions in Official Examination
Statement Is Held Warning to Bears

May 30, 1931

Trade Upturn Now Definite, Farrell Finds
Worst Slump Is Over, U. S. Steel Chief Declares, as
   Convention Closes

SUMMARY—INVESTMENT POLICY

1. If the long term trends of business activity and business profits are to be upward in the future as they have been upward in the past, depression zones should be utilized for the augmentation of common stock portfolios.

2. Any set of principles built upon the assumption that the average common stock investor will be entirely out of common stocks during a primary bear market, with his stock fund on deposit in the bank or invested only in gilt edge senior securities, is sheer nonsense.

Such an assumption is of scant value even from the theoretical standpoint, and of no value from the practical standpoint. Public psychology invalidates this assumption; the facts themselves invalidate it.

3. Similarly nonsensical is the assumption that the average common stock investor will be able to make

[272]

his depression-time accumulations at, or even close to, the absolute trough of a bear movement.

Although a broad depression possesses numerous distinguishing characteristics, there is no way of identifying positively the actual bottom of a major stock price down-swing, any more than there is a way by which one can with assurance identify the exact high point on a major bull swing.

Hence, in the earlier outline of our hypothetical investor's program during the 1930–1931 depression, we have allowed him to make several glaring mistakes—or at least have allowed him to take several steps which, in the light of facts now known, appear as mistakes at least for the time being.

To emphasize the principles involved, we have tried to show that these mistakes were more or less justified, in view of what the average investor was able to know or calculate at the time his steps were taken; we have further pointed to the penalties which were incurred, and have judged such penalties to be among the inescapable hazards of a long term common stock investment program.

4. The only logical or practical assumption, therefore, is that the average common stock owner went into the 1929–1931 bear market holding more stocks than he should have held, measured by results that were ticked off in his own pocketbook, and that he

[273]

continuously held throughout this movement more stocks than he should have carried down.

Our present concern, of course, is not solely or even primarily with the average common stock owner. It is with the average *business man investor:* the informed and intelligent investor who is willing, presumably, to be continuously studying his investment position; who is economically literate; who, as nearly as possible, approaches his problem from the scientific point of view.

This mitigates his situation, but does not entirely heal it. We must assume—as we already have done —that even this informed investor carried, on the average, more common stocks through the 1929– 1931 bear market than was good for his pocketbook. But in this case it is allowable to assume, we feel, that some sales, perhaps even substantial in volume, were effected during the summer and autumn of 1929. This releases a cash fund with which to rebuild.

5. The conservative investor would have resolutely resolved to retain a substantial portion of his free cash for employment in common stocks after improvement in business became a reality.

He would have realized quite well that, at such a time, average prices would be well above their absolute bottom level. This would not have concerned him in the slightest. He wanted insurance

[274]

and was willing to pay for it. In other words, he wanted to purchase some of his stocks too late.

6. This section of the program does not preclude our hypothetical investor from striving to make some of his additional purchases at or somewhere quite near the absolute bear bottom. It merely precludes him from risking too much of his money on his guess as to when the nadir had been reached.

Therefore, he will not only look forward to the prospect of buying some stocks too late, but likewise to the prospect of buying some too soon. His salvation is his moderation—if he has the courage and the vision to exercise it. Therefore he will buy, moderately, when actual prices appeal to him as really attractive, when the general situation is tending toward improvement, or when he can discover the real economic basis for *forecasting* probable near term improvement.

7. If he is fortunate enough to realize that his calculations as to future probabilities have been faulty, have contained an over-generous margin of error, he will correct his mistake, as promptly as possible, by some selling.

But note too that this selling, like our investor's previous piecemeal buying, will be moderate in volume. He will not *dare* sell too heavily. When he gets ready to take his action he will find it as difficult to make a decisive forecast as to impending ill as he would earlier have found it difficult to make a positive forecast of impending good. The uncertainties on both sides will dictate his moderation.

Quite decisively it should be asserted that successive buying and selling operations, either on the way up in a bull swing, or on the way down in a bear swing, do not constitute trading operations. As will be pointed out later, long term investment in common stocks does not mean doing nothing for the long term. It merely means being involved, as a partner, in business enterprises over a period of years. Intelligent business men strive to correct their mistakes as promptly as they are realized; intelligent common stock investors do likewise, regardless of whether their action applies to an individual stock, a group of stocks, or an aggregate situation.

It may also be urged that in the foregoing there is a certain amount of inconsistency. We have pointed out why the investing public as a whole cannot sell its stocks at bull peaks nor buy them back again at bear troughs; someone must carry them in the meanwhile, for better or for worse. Why then, it may be asked, is it consistent to talk about a depression-time accumulation policy which takes into account certain readjustments in position somewhere near the tops and bottoms of *intermediate, or shorter term, swings?*

We do not assume that *all* investors will do so, any more than we assume that *all* investors will sell some of their stocks near the peaks of bull swings, or be in a position to buy more near the bottoms of bear swings. But we do have a right to assume, we believe, that a considerable number of informed investors will do so; the movement of the market itself proves that they do. And we confidently look forward to the time when a much larger body of investors will so act, believing that the increasing pressure of such readjustments in investment position will be entirely good; that it will tend to level out these shorter swings, thereby inspiring a more sane public psychology.

8. The program outlined in the foregoing is believed to be applicable, in its broader terms, to the average typical business depression period. It means accumulating additional stocks in times of depression at prices considerably above the absolute low; it means doing some buying too soon, and some too late; it allows for the possibility of doing some buying at almost the right time, or at least striving to do so.

It means coming to the end of a depression with more cash than one should have. No apologies are offered for such a suggestion; no apologies need ever be offered for any suggestion which has as its objective the conservation of investment capital.

And, if cyclical recovery ever *does* come, the mistakes which were seemingly made by our hypothetical investor during his depression-time accumulation, will turn out to have been more apparent than real. The prices registered in the next major bull market, and the income returns derivative from good common stocks in the next period of prosperity, will be something quite different from what the average investor was envisioning in the dark, bleak summer of 1931— if the economic development of the United States is actually to continue over a period of years.

5. OTHER WAYS OF HEDGING THE PRICE-VALUE RISK

A. The Long Term Range of Operation

In the introduction to this study we were obliged to define the expression "long term" in a preliminary way, merely to give some general idea of the conception that was being dealt with. For simplicity, we put the idea wholly on a time basis, asserting that a long term investment operation is one undertaken by an investor who intends to hold his position for, say, a year or more.

We are now ready for a much more carefully stated, a much more precise definition.

A long term investment operation, as the expression is here used, is one undertaken by an investor who expects to hold his position (*a*) as long as the situation in which he has purchased a partnership promises further improvement, or increase in value or (*b*) until the price hazard has become so great that he feels he can no longer afford the luxury of partnership in this particular situation.

It will be instantly obvious that this conception of the long term investment operation is considerably more complex than the preliminary one that was set forth. It will also be observed that it is hardly the conventional definition.

For the most part our definition is self-explanatory, and needs only the minimum amount of further explanation.

According to the first qualification, when you purchase say five hundred shares of the common stock of the United States Steel Corporation, you do so with the expectation (if you are a long term investor) of retaining that stock in your strong box as long as you reaffirm the forecast that the intrinsic value of the United States Steel Corporation as a going business concern is likely to increase—*i.e.*, as long as the earnings available for your stock are likely to increase, and as long as dividends payable to you are likely to increase.

In this respect, the difference between the long term viewpoint and the short term one is mainly that the long term viewpoint is willing to look ahead for a period of time—perhaps for a period of years. It does not demand that earnings shall steadily increase month by month, nor quarter by quarter, and indeed, does not necessarily demand that earnings shall increase regularly year by year.

In other words, the long term viewpoint envisions a situation which is going to tend toward improvement over a period of years—a situation in which the long term trend is upward.

There are three main reasons why one would reverse one's viewpoint and sell:

a. Development of evidence that a mistake had been made in the investor's original analysis;

b. Development of outside and previously incalculable and unpredictable forces tending to change the direction of the established or estimated trend line;

c. Development of evidence of an impending major cyclical change, either in business in the aggregate, or in a particular industrial division of business. (As previously noted, most investors will not believe the warnings of an impending cyclical down-swing when they see them, so the selling occasioned by these phenomena is relatively small in volume. And be it noted that, if a stock is to be carried through a full cyclical down-swing, the type of issue best suited to that kind of tenacity is the one which has so definitely established an upward trend line that, at the peak of forthcoming Cycle *B*, its intrinsic value stands a better than average change to be measurably greater than at the peak of Cycle *A*, which lies just behind.)

Once the long pull investor has discovered that he has made a mistake in his analysis, or, to put it both more crudely and more expressively, that he has "picked a lemon," once he has discovered that forces which he had not previously allowed for have invalidated his forecast, or once he has definitely forecast a major cyclical down-swing in general business activity and therefore wants to heave a certain amount of ballast overboard, *he acts promptly and decisively.*

He doesn't fuss around waiting for a bulge that will give him a few more possible price points. He doesn't hem and haw; he doesn't temporize. *He sells.*

The most common mistake that is made relative to the long term operation is that the expression is used as a synonym for perseverance or stubbornness. The astute long term investor stays by his commitment as long as things go well, or as long as there is real reason to believe that the trend of value over a period of time will be decisively upward. He abandons his position when this becomes no longer a reasonable probability.

Long term operation does not mean becoming wedded to a stock. It does not mean the mere ability to hold on in the same way that a bulldog holds on. *It means tenacity and singleness of purpose only so long as the forecast of a further increase in intrinsic value is a reasonable probability.*

There are several thousand issues of active common stock available to American investors;

many, many thousands of unlisted ones. When the long pull investor finds he is "stymied" with the issue or issues he is holding, the only sensible course is to abandon his old position, and take a new one. He always has a wide choice.

Thus a certain amount of market activity is in no wise inconsistent with the strictly long term viewpoint. The investor is constantly searching for the ideal common stock investment: the issue that will increase in value at the most rapid rate, *ad infinitum*. He never finds it; sometimes he remains so far away from it that it seems an infinitely distant star. But the one certain thing is that he will get nowhere at all with his program if, because of stubbornness, ignorance, or what not, he keeps a sizable portion of his funds tied up in issues the long term trends of which are downward or sidewise, rather than upward.

The most important thing to bear in mind is that long term trends change slowly. The change in a trend line is not discovered by a genius-like flash of intuition, but by careful study over a period of time. The investor needs to be very cautious, therefore, about acting too precipitately; there is always the temptation to be jumping in and out of situations if a forecast that has been made does not mature immediately.

In other words, there is a temptation to do a considerable amount of actual trading, under the guise of "readjusting long term position." This totally destroys the advantages of the long term method of operation.

We believe there are certain circumstances under which the long term investor will do well to consider surrendering his position in a given stock *on the basis of price alone.*

Obviously, the price hazard increases (*i.e.,* the danger of a serious collapse in price increases) as price draws farther and farther away from earnings. Somewhere on the scale upward there is a zone of real danger for the average investor—a point at which current price would seem, on the basis of any sensible analysis, to discount all that could be hoped for, in the development of intrinsic value, for years and years to come. An abnormally high price-earnings ratio, and an abnormally low yield if the stock is on a dividend basis, are usually the symptoms of this situation.

Quite aside from the fact that, at such a price level, the investor is receiving a low income return on his money, the stock that he is carrying becomes a real luxury. If in this particular issue he is forced to lay out twenty-five to thirty dollars for one dollar in earnings, with the *average* first grade stock available on a considerably more reasonable basis, he is paying a fancy price—and, patently, a fancy price for the privilege of carrying an increasingly heavy hazard.

His purchase price has nothing whatsoever to do with it. That is past, forgotten. Today's current price tells him how much money he has tied up in a particular situation. His investment is today's price times the number of shares he is carrying. His only question is whether that sum of money, as reported by today's price, is working the way he wants it to work.

It is obviously impossible to lay down arbitrary standards as to what price-earnings ratio, or what yield, constitutes a signal that a price hazard has been carried into a danger zone. With reference back to the earlier discussion of these two factors, we can only repeat that somewhere in the price scale there is a level at which the danger of continuing to carry is inconsistent with the risk involved and that, in such cases, the long term investor may well give consideration to abandoning his position on a price basis alone—abandoning it to go into some other more conservatively priced situation, or to await until the particular one that has frightened him is again priced more reasonably.

What are the chief advantages of the long term method of operation?

1. It is infinitely simpler than any other. A long term trend is easier to forecast than a short term trend.

2. This is especially true in an economy in which the dominant trend for business in the aggregate moves in a constant direction. (*Example:* the long term *upward* trend in the American economy.)

3. The long term operation is based upon analysis rather than upon guess.

4. It is geared mainly to value analysis, and only incidentally or occasionally to the estimation of the proper relation of price to value, and therewith tends to eliminate or at least minimize the harmful possibilities of the most irrational factor in the joint price-value risk.

5. It can afford to ignore the short term movements, both in value and in price. Therefore these short term movements are not allowed to become confusing, nor to obscure the basic forecast.

6. It provides insurance against the unnecessary loss of a position in a given stock.

7. It has "the growth of the country" and the dominating trend of public psychology working for it, rather than against it, the greater part of the time.

8. It is the reasonable method of operation for the conservative investor. (This is a statement of opinion; not an argument.)

B. CREDIT POLICIES

More investment programs have been wrecked by ill-advised credit policies than by any other single factor.

For some unexplainable reason, the average investor appears to regard security market credit as quite distinct and separate from other kind of credit. He regards it as credit that can easily be paid back if stocks go up in price, *but the unfortunate thing is that stocks do not always go up.*

Even in an economy where the long term secular trend is upward, stock prices sometimes go down. An incredible fact, in certain periods and according to certain habits of thought; but none the less an inescapable one. And when prices do move downward in a cyclical movement thay have an unhappy habit of moving downward quite rapidly.

The lender is not interested in the especial problems of Investor *A*, *B* or *C*. He is interested in the return of 100 per cent of the principal that he has loaned. When he sees developments that threaten the safety of that principal, he uses the discretion that is implicit in a call loan. Holding the collateral, the lender sells the borrower out. For this line of action there is no basis of criticism, except from the standpoint of the borrower. And his viewpoint dosn't matter, so long as the lender has discretionary powers.

[287]

The important permanent losers in the 1929–1931 stock market debacle were those who were carrying unduly heavy loans. The decline in stock values was greater than their equities. When the smoke of the battlefield cleared, they found they had *nothing* left. Some of them had debts, because the lenders could not sell fast enough, but for our present purposes we will consider minus quantities as the equivalent of zero.

Principles:

1. Few business men make progress comparable with their ambitions if they employ in their business enterprises only their savings.

2. They customarily utilize a considerable volume of borrowed funds.

3. If their enterprises are successful, the use of the other fellow's money greatly enhances their profits.

4. A collateral loan is not, fundamentally, different from any other kind of a loan. Certainly, no greater degree of opprobrium attaches to a collateral loan than to any other kind.

5. Least of all is a collateral loan different from any other kind of a loan in the characteristics of its maturity. A collateral loan, like all others, must be paid back.

6. The wisest security purchaser is the one who does not carry a larger collateral loan than he can pay back, without undue strain, if his expectations of market performance are not fulfilled.

7. The hazard in security market operation tends to increase directly as the margin of credit involved in that transaction increases.

8. Conversely, the hazard is reduced as the margin of credit involved is reduced.

9. The operator who is employing only his own funds cannot conceivably be sold out. He cannot suffer anything other than a "paper loss." If he has the right kind of stocks, and if the long term trend of business activity continues upward, this loss must not only be ultimately restored, but upon it there must be compounded a subsequent profit.

C. DIVERSIFICATION

Diversification in the portfolio is insurance against errors in judgment. Ten sails get more wind than five sails—twenty more than ten.

No individual's judgment can be 100 per cent correct. No line of analysis extending into the future can conceivably be 100 per cent correct, or anything approaching that figure.

Diversification to some extent atones for the inevitable errors—*i.e.*, intelligent diversification does so: diversification among the situations that seem most likely to go forward the most rapidly.

[289]

Over-diversification is a common fault. Under-diversification is an equally common one. In all the foregoing a consistent effort has been made to avoid arbitrary mathematical statements. For the moment this effort will be discarded, but more in the interest of definiteness than in the spirit of dictation.

The $100,000 common stock account can readily carry twenty-five different issues.

The $1,000,000 account can readily carry fifty to sixty issues.

No account should carry a greater number of issues than the owner can carefully watch, at all times.

D. Radical and Conservative Issues

A conservative issue is one which may be carried in the portfolio with the minimum risk that is consistent with the possibilities of gain.

With such issues, the chances are better than average that the long term trend is upward. For instance, there is scant room for doubt that some-time during the next five years the United States Steel Corporation will sell more steel, and at better prices, than it sold in 1930; that General Motors will sell more automobiles; that American Can will sell more containers; that Standard Oil of New Jersey will sell more gasoline; that Endicott-Johnson will sell more shoes.

The possibility that any of these corporations will treble or quadruple its earnings during the next five years, however, is quite remote.

The radical issues are the longer chances—the ones which the odds are against but which, if they manage to make the grade, have simply tremendous profit-making possibilities. Neon lights, television, certain steel alloys, air transportation, new electrical devices based upon the resolving of matter into its atomic parts—these things have unlimited possibilities. If an investor held a position in a half dozen of them, and if only one achieved its ultimate possibilities, the other five could be written off as a total loss, and still a handsome profit would be achieved. Some of the radio companies went through this miraculous cycle in 1928–1929. Unhappily, however, the subsequent collapse brought the investor down as near zero, on the average, as it is ever possible to get.

A common stock may constitute a radical commitment either on the basis of the value risk, or on the basis of the price risk. In view of what we know about the long term rate of growth in steel consumption, and of what we know about the overcapacity of the industry and the resultant effect upon the price structure, United States Steel common selling at 20 to 25 times earnings would certainly be a radical situation for the average investor to participate in, except at the bottom of a general business depression.

Once more we shall be arbitrary, more in the interest of a definite statement than otherwise.

The average investor will be skating on thin ice when more than 25 per cent of the current market value of his common stock portfolio is in radical commitments. In times of business depression, and in the culminating periods of frenzied booms, the proportion of radicals can be dropped well below 25 per cent, without much sacrifice of potential long term gain.

E. Possession and Utilization of Analytical Facilities

The first step in the common stock program is the selection of the individual stocks that are to go into the portfolio—the choosing of those specific issues which, over a period of time, will as closely as possible mirror the hypothetical performance of the ideal investment stock.

Value is the item of primary consideration in selection. Price is secondary, but a thoroughly important secondary element. At certain times it becomes, unhappily, a dominant element. The ideal is more nearly approached when it is a matter of reasonable expectation that, over a period of time, no extraneous forces will appear to prevent price from reflecting true value.

The second step in the program is the continuous watching of these selected stocks as individuals. This means regular gathering and analysis of new data as they become available; continuous reforecast; reselection as for one reason or another previously established positions are abandoned.

The third step is the continuous watching of the portfolio *as a whole*, against the possibility of developments of major consequences which may affect *all stocks horizontally*.

Needless to point out, this process of original selection, watching, selling, reselection, etc., requires something more than mere casual attention. It requires adequate fact-gathering facilities; adequate fact-analyzing and fact-projecting facilities.

The investor who is unwilling to set up his own system for the possession and utilization of such facilities has scant excuse for the role of a partner in business enterprise—*fluctuation* being a dominant characteristic not only of specific enterprise, but of enterprise in the aggregate.

The investor unwilling to assume the burdens involved in the necessitous program of fact gathering, analysis, and forecast will be much better off, in the long run, as a saver than as a partner in the business enterprise.

[293]

6. RESERVES

As has been pointed out, a common stock investment program is essentially a risk-bearing program. Even the most conservative situations are not without a generous measure of the risk element. It is a threefold risk: a risk geared to the major trend of aggregate business activity; to the trend of volume of production, selling prices, and margins of profit in a given line of business; to the successful management and good fortunes of a specific enterprise.

It is both proper and prudent that a reserve against these risks should be retained.

There are two distinct kinds of security account reserves: the temporary and the permanent. The temporary reserve is a reserve for the purchase of additional common stocks some time in the future —such as our wise investor carried through most of the 1930–1931 depression. It is a fluctuating amount, depending upon time and circumstance. Ultimately, it is *all* destined to go back into the common stock section of the portfolio.

The permanent reserve is the reserve in the security account *as a whole;* it constitutes that section of the account which is customarily employed in senior securities (bonds, preferred stocks, etc.) which promise steady income, but the minimum of either capital appreciation or depreciation. The risk is pared down to the bone, in other words, and the resultant penalty of low income return is cheerfully accepted.

The permanent reserve, too, is a fluctuating element.

In the conservatively operated account, it will fluctuate in one direction and in one direction only— *upward.* **It will be steadily augmented from profits that are won in common stocks, if any, or from income from other sources. It will not, except under the most extraordinary circumstances, be disturbed to compensate for common stock losses.**

It is this analyst's judgment that the temptation to try to make capital profit out of the permanent reserve fund should be sternly renounced. Such a program can only be successful over a period of time, if second or third grade bonds or preferred stocks are purchased. But the possibilities for gains in common stocks are so much greater than those for gains in second and third grade bonds and preferreds, that the risks involved in the lower-grade senior issues are simply not worth the candle.

The careful investor will do his speculating in common stocks, where the possible gain is at least

[295]

to some extent commensurate with the risk involved. He will see that, as nearly as is consistent with a moderate and reasonable income return, his permanent reserve account is virtually the equivalent of cash—and that it steadily grows.

7. "THE LIQUIDATION OF THE COMMON STOCK IDEA"

It is sometimes said that the trends of the world's affairs are not shaped so much by deeds as by words. This may be an exaggeration. But certainly at all times one observes the springing forth of catch phrases which gain wide currency, and which by their mere implications profoundly influence not only the habits of thought, but the actions, of great groups of men. This is especially true in Wall Street, where thinking is not always as profound as our philosophers might like to have it.

For example, as the great bull market of 1921–1929 marched unhaltingly toward its inevitable end, the term new era was dragged out and given a significance which it had never before possessed. It was on so many persons' tongues that, literally, we talked ourselves into the belief that we actually had arrived at a new economic era, and we acted accordingly—with the evil results that are now so well and painfully known.

In this "new era" the term equity security took on a new meaning. Everyone used it. It signified something much beyond what is signified by the lowly words common stock. If "common" was plebian, "equity" was high hat. No one took the trouble to draw nice distinctions, but if they had done so, it probably would have come to light that an equity security was an instrumentality through the possession of which anyone, no matter how humble, might share in the increasing profits of American business enterprise. The common conception made no allowance for the opportunity so offered to share in business losses. Equity and profits came to be generally synonymous. That, precisely, was why so many persons avidly desired equity securities.

In the summer of 1931, one of the neatest and at the same time one of the most popular phrases generously utilized among financially-minded people was "the liquidation of the common stock idea." This was merely another way of expressing the opinion that common stocks are not good long term investments. Thus, just as the equity craze had been the obsession of many minds as the previous major bull market had neared its peak, so the anti-equity obsession made swift headway as the succeeding bear market approached its bottom. A well-turned phrase was not without influence in both instances.

Now, this writer takes the position that, in the preceding pages, he has put his head into so many nooses, has hatched so many chickens which may later be coming home to roost, that he should be spared the crowning indiscretion of offering an opinion as to whether common stocks do or do not constitute good long term investments. A few brief concluding observations, however, which approach the answer but never entirely get there, may be allowable.

In the first place, the significance of the term "long term investment," as it is used in this study, is again pointed to, even at the risk of excessive tedium. An intelligent long term common stock investor is not a Rip Van Winkle. He does not purchase his common stocks and then go up in the mountains to fall asleep for twenty years. He works. He studies. He develops and utilizes specialized tools. He exposes himself to all of the economic information that is available, or at least all that he can absorb. He buys carefully chosen common stocks with the *intention* of holding for the long pull, but he does not hesitate to correct himself when he finds either (*a*) that he has made a mistake, or (*b*) that the situation in which he is committed no longer promises further improvement.

His economic knowledge in these matters, and his skill in working out his program may, conceivably, have an important bearing as to whether the common stocks which move in and out of his portfolio over a period of years constitute good or bad long term investments.

Whether it is "the general market" which one buys or disposes of at any given time, or scientifically studied individual stocks, may also conceivably have an important bearing upon long term results.

The extent to which any individual is committed in common stocks, at any time, should depend altogether upon the extent to which he conceives it proper and wise for him to be committed in business enterprise as an active partner.

This viewpoint, it seems to me, is of transcending importance in straight thinking about the common stock problem. Business enterprise in anything but a theoretical stabilized economy, automatically confers a financial risk. Some types of business enterprise offer the possibility of greater gains than others, and therewith confer greater risks; so likewise with common stocks.

Because the fractional partnerships in large business enterprises are actively traded in on organized markets, and because selling prices become a matter of record each day, the shares of these larger concerns carry a price hazard as well as a value hazard. But when contrast is made with the small, privately owned, non-liquid business concern, this disadvantage is more apparent than real. The difference between what a 100-car capacity garage and automobile repair shop could have been sold for in September, 1929, and what it could have been sold for in June, 1931, is probably not greatly dissimilar to the spread between the prices of General Motors common stock on these two dates. The fact that a depreciation in value is unrecorded does not change the factual aspects of the case.

Perhaps it will be urged that the small-sized partner in a big enterprise, as an absentee owner, is more likely to be the victim of chicanery of management, dilution of equity, knavery of bankers, price manipulation by heartless speculators, etc., than is the private owner of a small enterprise who is in a position to watch closely all of his eggs, and to control this small concern's policies.

It is possible that there is validity in this viewpoint. But I am not prepared to admit it. A number of years of contacts with all kinds and degrees of business men has utterly failed to convince this observer that big business men are more dishonest or less competent than little business men on the average, or that big bankers are any sharper in their dealings than small bankers, or that big financiers have any different code whatsoever from small financiers. Indeed, a great deal could be said on the *other* side of the question.

[301]

The economic structure represents business enterprise all along the line. The difference is one of degree rather than of fact; of the technique in which ownership of enterprise is distributed and held. The purchaser and seller of common stocks assumes a business risk, just as do all other business men who place their funds in business enterprise of any kind. It remains to be proved that liquidity of the partnership imposes a hardship that is not thoroughly compensated for in other ways. The investor's decision as to whether he shall or shall not carry fractional partnerships in his portfolio turns, in the final analysis, upon the degree in which he feels justified in assuming, or in desperation feels obliged to assume, the risk of business enterprise.

The hypothesis that the long term trend of prosperity is to be upward in the United States in the future as it has been upward over the long term past, has been accepted for this study, as previously stated. In the summer of 1931 the acceptance of such a principle might be regarded by many persons as an act of great courage, harking back again to the daring habits of thought of the "new era."

As a matter of fact, the theory of long term economic growth is the only possible one which commends itself to common sense. It may be that this is the time that the opposing theory is to

[302]

become valid; but if so, there is at this time nothing in the world but sheer blind guess to point to the establishment of any right-about revision in principle. All experience, all of the technique of economic reasoning which we have learned, throw their weight to the growth theory.

So far as the stock market phase of this theory is concerned, it is built up step by step as follows:

1. It is held that the long term trend of the per capita volume of our physical production is upward —perhaps at a slackening rate of gain, and subject to cyclical interruptions of various lengths, but upward nevertheless.

2. With rising volume, commodity prices will usually take care of themselves.

3. Therefore, the long term trend of business profits is upward, profits being a derivative of the product of volume and prices.

4. Therefore, the long term trend of common stock values is upward, and finally,

5. Therefore, the long term trend of common stock prices is upward.

This, in its briefest possible form of statement, is the theory which has been here accepted in the absence of any more reasonable one. Likewise, one accepts the theories that larger masses of matter attract smaller ones in this universe of ours; that the sum of the squares of the legs of a right-angle triangle is equal to the square of the hypotenuse; that light does not travel in a straight line; that the moon, having no atmosphere, is uninhabitable, etc. In no case does acceptance involve a guarantee, but if anyone disputes any of these principles which science has taught us to fit into our conception of the universe, we have the right to feel that the burden of proof is upon them rather than upon ourselves.

It is a fact almost too obvious to call for restatement that if the long term trend of American business prosperity *is* upward, then the *average* common stock is a good long term investment—the phrase long term investment, of course, being subject to the qualifications laid down for the purposes of this study.

If the long term trend of business prosperity is sidewise from the current level, then not the average common stock, but only a minority of them (those able to increase their profits while the majority are standing still) will constitute good long term investments.

If the long term business trend is downward, then only the very exceptional common stock is a good long term investment.

Finally, if over the long term future only the minority of common stocks, or, worse still, only the very exceptional ones are to be good long term investments, then what are we to say of the prospect for the hundreds of thousands of smaller, privately owned businesses? Have we any reason whatsoever to assume that the trend of profits of the average small business is going to be upward, or even horizontal, while the trend of the profits of the average large scale enterprise is moving downward? Do fractional partnerships confer so great a penalty over integral ownerships?

The truth of the matter is that if the time has now arrived to "liquidate the common stock idea," it has arrived coincidentally with the time to liquidate the idea of being in business in any way. The fortunes of public and private ownership must move together.

If the liquidators of the common stock idea are right in their premise—and nothing herein disputes that they *may* be right—then they have only begun their appointed task when they have liquidated this particular idea. They would better go ahead and liquidate the savings idea as well, because on a long term downward trend of business profits the washing away of common stock equities would be only the beginning; the next—and absolutely inevitable—step would be the elimination, or at best the partial destruction of the savers' underlying equity in our economic establishment.

On the other hand, if the phrase "liquidating the common stock idea" should by any chance suggest the desirability of liquidating the dangerous kinds of viciously reckless thinking about the common stock problem which disclose themselves at bull market crests and at bear market troughs . . . then the quicker we get about this part of the business, the better.